THE IMPRACTICAL BOAT OWNER

Dave Selby

Illustrated by Jake Kavanagh

D1440189

ADLARD COLES NAUTICAL

OOMSBURY

OXFORD • NEW YORK • NEW DELHI • SYDNEY

Adlard Coles Nautical
An imprint of Bloomsbury Publishing Plc

50 Bedford Square
London
WC1B 3DP
UK

1385 Broadway
New York
NY 10018
USA

www.bloomsbury.com
www.adlardcoles.com

ADLARD COLES, ADLARD COLES NAUTICAL and the Buoy logo
are trademarks of Bloomsbury Publishing Plc

First published 2017

British Library Cataloguing-in-Publication Data
A catalogue record for this book is available from the British Library.

Library of Congress Cataloguing-in-Publication data has been applied for.

ISBN: PB: 978-1-4729-4484-9
        ePDF: 978-1-4729-4483-2
        ePub: 978-1-4729-4485-6

10 9 8 7 6 5 4 3

Design and additional images by Bradbury & Williams
Printed and bound by Bell & Bain Ltd., Glasgow G46 7UQ

MIX
Paper from
responsible sources
FSC® C007785

To find out more about our authors and books visit www.bloomsbury.com.
Here you will find extracts, author interviews, details of
forthcoming events and the option to sign up for our newsletters.

Photographs: page 5 © Dave Selby; page 112 © Julie George

CONTENTS

INTRODUCTION

The publishers of this book just don't get it. They thought it would be full of ingenious tip-top top tips and handy 'cut out and keep' how-to guides. Well, they asked the wrong guy. Nevertheless they insisted, and I hoodwinked them by offering to insert some totally bogus 'Lessons Learned'.

These are a regular feature of most sailing magazines, except for the racing ones, because racy sailors know it all and never actually learn anything; otherwise they wouldn't still be doing it. In other mags, 'Lessons Learned' generally appear at the end of those gruesome first-hand reader accounts designed to show how terrifying, dangerous and unpleasant sailing is. Such catastrophes usually take place in a gale so fierce the proud boat owner couldn't persuade a photographer to come out in a RIB and snap the biblical horror. And this is why these articles are illustrated by a painting of the grim scene, which is then given to the author as a memento. In fact, I'm constantly amazed at the lengths people will go to for a painting of their boat.

Sailing, as we know, is all about suffering, and at the end of their lurid articles, in 'Lessons Learned' the authors set about beating themselves up with the relish of a Jesuit priest, cataloguing their lifetime failings, character flaws and faults in a litany of lifelong underachievement. And then they buy dozens of copies of the magazine to show off their self-flagellation to all their chums. This makes sound financial publishing sense as it boosts magazine circulation.

The fact is there is nothing practical about sailing whatsoever. That's the whole point. Sailing is sublimely pointless, magnificently impractical – and I'm the very living embodiment of that. That's why you won't learn anything from my 'Lessons Learned'. That's a promise.

You see, I'm lucky. I came to sailing late in life and although I've been sailing now for over 15 years I haven't learned much – and that's what gives me so much to write about. Indeed, the accompanying picture tells you all you need to know about my limited capabilities. This is without doubt the high point of my sailing career, and at least I had the foresight to be towing my tender, from which I took this pic of *Marlin*, my Sailfish 18. That's a tip-top top tip.

It's my sincere hope that you won't learn anything from this book, because not all things need answers. The wind and waves still mystify me, the workings of the weather too, and I thank the stars I haven't lost the wonder. Perhaps sailing means too much to me, but then it's taught me so many things and none of them has anything to do with sailing.

For sure I know more of myself; I think I'm a better person, kinder, rounder, fuller, deeper, easier to be with, a better shipmate, a better friend, with even better friends. The sea did that, and my wonderful little Sailfish 18. And I dream of boats and voyages yet to come.

These days I'm a man on a mission: Marlin's Mission, it's called, and the idea is to show that cost is no barrier to getting afloat, and to raise money for my charity. In 2012 I became ill with a rare viral condition called Guillain-Barré syndrome. It's an illness of the peripheral nervous system and, in my case, it means the messages stop getting through to my legs every four weeks or so; then, over three days, antibodies from the blood of 800 donors restore my legs. Humbling.

And I'm humbled also by my friends who got me back on the water when I'd lost confidence. Grateful too, for the illness turned into a blessing and gave me the nudge I needed. Marlin's Mission continues, and I hope you'll keep me company along the way, for you're the best crewmates this bloke could wish for.

Dave Selby, www.impracticalboatowner.com, Maldon, Essex
www.facebook.com/impracticalboatowner
www.justgiving.com/Dave-Selby-Marlins-Mission

A BAD CASE OF FENDER ENVY

'He's either got a Sunseeker Predator or he's compensating for something...'

Real boat owners don't know, or maybe can't remember, how much it hurts not to own a boat.

You've had a great day's sail and you can be doing just fine, enjoying bar-room bonhomie and banter with fellow Musto'd-up salts. The warmth you feel, you don't know if it's from fellowship, the fire or the mulled wine. Wherever you are, in a musty yacht club or dive pub, it's a great place to be. You belong.

Then someone asks you what boat you own. Aaaaagh! It's the question that pierces the non-boat owner to the quick. The fire fizzles out, ice forms on the beer and tumbleweeds blow through the bar. You've been exposed. Suddenly you feel like a desperate hanger-on, an outsider, inadequate.

That's how I always felt – until early last year. It was February: I'm frozen, the wind is whipping across North Weald Aerodrome, but I'm warm inside as I queue up for the Essex Boat Jumble.

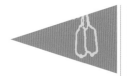

I've just become the proudest boat owner there's ever been, and justifiably so. Of course, there are wrong-minded folk who think there are ugly caravans prettier than my 18-and-a-half-foot Sailfish, but beauty is in the eye of the boat owner. And for a couple of grand I reckon my little sloop is a budget brown-water classic. I want everyone to know she's mine, all mine.

I haggle over a scrap of rope and, as I hand my 30p to the ungrateful stallholder, announce, 'It's for my Sailfish.' I splash out £2.50 on a brand-new PP9 battery for my antique echo sounder and manage to slip in that 'it's for my Sailfish'. My next opportunity for a statement of boat ownership costs £24, for a pair of cockpit cushions. This is getting reckless.

Then I spot the fenders and can no longer contain my urge to lay objects of devotion before my loved one. Naturally, I inform the stone-faced stallholder that the fenders are 'for my Sailfish'. I'd like to buy the lot, but restrict myself to six, at £5 a pop. I can't wait to garland my Sailfish with these little lozenges of love. But that must wait.

I suspect there are still a few among the thousands at the boat jumble who don't know I'm a boat owner. I drape my pint-pot fenders over my shoulders and go for a swagger. You see, fenders are far more than nautical kneepads; they can speak, and what they announce to the world is that you actually own a boat, for who would buy fenders without owning a boat? They'd have to be daft. These little pods, barely larger than dung-beetle larvae, are my passport to the inner circle, my badge of belonging to the group of 'we boat owners'.

As I swagger to my car, all aflush, fenders jiggling on my shoulders, I'm stopped dead in my tracks by a truly horrible sight: a man with bigger fenders than mine! They're not just big, each one is almost the size of my Sailfish. Aaaaagh! I'm struck down

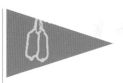

with fender envy, 'cos you know what they say about blokes with big fenders: 'Big fenders, big boat; small fenders, small boat.'

Still, if anyone scoffs at the size of my fenders, I'll just say they're for my tender. That should puncture their ego.

Lessons ~~Not~~ Learned

None really. They say every day's a school day, but I didn't turn up much, which is why I fell into the underpaid unskilled trade of journalism, which pays even less if you write about boats for 'Impractical Boat Owner', which is why I can't afford a proper boat. Neither can my poor colleagues on Practical Boat Owner, which is why they spend all their time trying to keep their derelict fleet afloat with Sellotape and Dairylea cartons. Their despair and penury fills a magazine that enables their perma-tanned bosses to keep their superyachts in the Caribbean. Occasionally they allow the PBO team to anti-foul or polish their superyachts for a magazine feature; this makes them shiny, stops crud sticking to the hulls and renders them tax-deductible. So it turns out the perma-tans are the most practical of all. Not that I'm resentful.

COMPETENT
SCREW-UPS

'No, it's not a storm job, they're my husband's underpants.'

I was standing in the early-morning drizzle, one leg bent, the other outstretched as I leaned my body into the soft breeze, looking skyward and licking the water off my face.

'Is that yoga? Why don't you come in for breakfast?' my friend Angie called from the house. That was the moment I knew I'd got it bad. I was standing in her garden in an odd slanted pose, intently studying the neighbour's washing line, trying to figure out which was the main halyard and whether the bed linen could be sheeted in a little more tightly. Thankfully there was no lingerie on the line – that could have been embarrassing.

I'd just returned from my first week on board a yacht and had a signed certificate to prove it. What it should have said, in bold script along the bottom, was 'WARNING! Sailing is extremely contagious', because my world had turned upside down. It was like 'Alice through the porthole'. Sleeping in a bed felt odd, the

ground didn't move, and being inside, even when it was raining, was like being in a fairground ride where the walls and floor close in on you. The oddest thing was looking up at the sky and seeing only ceiling.

And just five days before all this I'd been pretty normal, more or less. As I stepped on board the Jeanneau 35 in Southampton's Ocean Village there was the faintest tremor of movement beneath my feet, nothing more, the boat's living pulse setting up a synchronisation signal with mine.

That night I never slept a wink. It was real, clammy terror. I could hear the ominously gentle *ploop, ploop* of water licking along the hull inches from my ear. Was the water level on the outside getting higher because of something I'd done on the inside? I'd used the toilet, but I really wasn't qualified – all those levers and pumps. I'd also used the sink, but had I done it right? It wouldn't look good if I killed everyone – including me – before we even untied the boat.

In the morning the skipper stepped on board knowing nothing of my torment. With long wispy white hair, sandals, Levi 501s, tie-dye T-shirt and John Lennon specs he looked every inch the regulation old hippy; later we learned he'd swapped one uniform for another. He'd been an officer in the marines, had served in the Falklands and took up sailing only when he retired. Mostly he was the model of calm, patience, but just occasionally, when we messed up real good, his eyes would turn to gimlets and bore into our souls. Just for a fleeting second it seemed he was going to screech 'You 'orrible shower' and have us stand to attention on the spreaders in our underwear.

My recall of the first days is hazy. I was too anxious and over-eager, trying not to kill everybody. The rest of the time was divided between tripping over, ducking and closing sea cocks (they've

become something of a passion). Slowly I started to relax and the fear gave way to wonder; and nothing was more wondrous than the night passage, as our small boat became a speck on the edge of a planet that was a speck in a twinkling universe.

Then there were lovely light moments, most memorably when fellow novice Kevin and I were on the foredeck and the skipper shouted, 'Lasso that buoy!' Well, the skipper might just as well have said, 'Hi ho, Silver, away!' It sounded like cowboy talk and we had not a clue what relevance the words had to the boathook and tangle of ropes we had in our hands. We looked at each other blankly and all I could think to do was say to Kevin in the style of John Wayne, 'That'll be the day.' As the buoy kissed the bow and slipped by, we collapsed in pleats of laughter and didn't even see the skipper's gimlet eyes bore through us. Then the two crewmates in the cockpit caught the laughter, the skipper too, and the whole boat giggled.

When it was all over and I was back home, I realised something. I realised that I ached to be back on a boat, to learn how to sail, something so simple that a leaf on a pond knows how to do it, yet remains a miracle to me. Today, a couple of years on, that wonder still remains, and so too many of the eternal mysteries – sea cocks, for one.

LESSONS **NOT** LEARNED

Try to avoid the wide-eyed, sickly sentimentality expressed in this highly irresponsible article. If not, you might end up buying a boat.

CONFUSED ABOUT WHICH BOAT TO BUY?
THIS WON'T HELP

'Drop keels are great! Did you notice how SOFTLY it went down?'

I really feel it's about time the government – or a higher authority such as the RYA – stepped in to regulate the predatory and irresponsible IFA industry. These days, all you need to do is glance sidelong at the water and it won't be long before an IFA sidles up and taps your elbow. I've even seen the more aggressive IFAs lie in wait for puddles to form and hold motivational seminars around osmosis blisters. It's got to stop.

IFAs, by the way, are not Independent Financial Advisers but Independent Floatation Advisers. Most of them will also give financial advice, but mostly they exist to perplex the would-be

boat owner into taking up golf. Just whisper that one day you might possibly perhaps be kind of considering thinking about maybe buying a boat and the global IFA community mobilises en masse.

The ones who own boats tell you to get ones like theirs – presumably because they either want you to share their disappointment or want to sell you theirs. Wiser yet are the ones who used to own boats and consequently can give you the benefit of a whole series of mistakes. But others, most sagely of all, have by their own admission never owned boats and smugly proclaim themselves members of the OPYC, the Other People's Yacht Club. These are the ones who brag of how they get all their sailing for free, and they usually have particular insight into which boats have the largest, fastest drinks-chilling capability; ashore they can be found close to the bar but never quite within reach of their own pocket.

With all that help it soon became clear that I should get a single-masted ketch – or possibly yawl – with a long-keeled centre-plate shoal-draught deep fin with swinging bilge keels and lee boards. It should also be as big as I could afford, while being the smallest possible boat that gave the space I needed. Other than that, a brand-new boat would always make its money back, while you'd also be quids in with an older boat that had already given away most of its depreciation. There was even one bloke who said I should get a wooden boat. What madness!

I listened to them all and, in truth, they all helped because what they were really telling me was to listen to myself. By then I'd become addicted to classified ads and discovered that for two to three grand there was a vast armada of small GRP boats that could get me into more than enough trouble.

As I'd be plying the shallow, thick brown ooze around the River Blackwater on the Essex coast, the ideal craft would probably be

a BMW 4x4. Unfortunately even rough ones are more than three grand, so I faced a compromise. Charts being what they are, I knew that if I bought anything with a fixed-fin or long keel I'd be spending most of my time on my side. And bilge keelers, it seems to me, are good at going aground upright and staying there. It was then that I saw my first Sailfish 18, high and dry on a mound of sand like a cherry crowning a Bakewell tart. Here was a boat that clearly excelled at going aground – but how? A quick £3.50 to the *PBO* Copy Service for a copy of David Harding's used-boat test revealed the secret. The ballasted vertically lifting keel winds right up into the hull, reducing draft from 3ft to 1ft. This seemed ideal; when they've put the land in the wrong place, you just wind 'n' go.

But all these keel considerations are really beside the point. In my short time afloat I've been saddened to come across so many boat owners whose pleasure often seems far outweighed by the heavy burden of ownership. What I've really learned by diving in and buying a boat of my own choosing is that I really enjoy boat ownership. And when a lesson like that costs only two grand I call it a bargain. Hello, mud, here I come!

LESSONS NOT LEARNED

Don't listen to anyone, especially someone who raves about their own boat. Either they're trying to sell it or they want you to share their grief.

YOU CANNOT BE CIRRUS!

'Now here is the shipping forecast...'
'My God! Just look at those isobars!'

The weather does my head in. I've been to the night classes and bought the books. I've even opened them, but that just causes the build up of a nasty high-pressure system at the front of my skull, followed by a deep low.

Still, I try my best to be prepared, so on the Monday before the weekend I'm going sailing I start gathering input to fill my deep well of murky incomprehension: radio and VHF shipping forecasts, premium-rate text messages and phone forecasts. By Friday, with the aid of synoptic charts printed off the internet and fax, I've got enough paisley swirls to wallpaper a double bedroom. And still I've got no idea whether to go sailing or buy wallpaper paste. If this carries on the most likely long-term outlook is that I'll have to sell my boat to pay for the weather forecasts.

Still, I'm learning and the one big thing I've learned is what I don't know, if that makes sense. I've also come to the conclusion that you can know too much. I know a sailor who knows so much about the weather that he talks mostly in Latin. He'll cast an eye at the sky, nod with the wisdom of the ages and quietly and confidently intone something like 'Habeas corpus cumulonimbus spirito sancti.' There's no doubt he's an expert, because on the odd occasions he resorts to English, it makes even less sense: 'If clouds look as if scratched by a hen, get ready to reef your topsails then.' I look up and I see one cloud that looks a bit like a kangaroo, but most of the clouds I've come across look like sheep. This gentleman sailor is so in tune with the elements that the whiskers of his luxuriant gaff-rigged moustache can detect the slightest changes in barometric pressure.

All of which gets me to wondering why I'm standing on the toe-rail, heaving my whole body weight against the wheel of his long-keeled blue-water beauty, as we career close-hauled with all sail up in an almighty blow. It was last November as the two of us attempted to bring his 36-foot cruiser down from Lowestoft in Suffolk. The day dawned bright and clear and as we sailed down the coast I was treated to so much softly intoned Latin I could almost smell the incense. Later we could have done with a priest to go with it.

Throughout the day the tale of the skies unfolded exactly as he'd foretold. His powers of prophecy were so awesome I began to wonder if he was not actually commanding the skies to do his bidding. I could feel the wind rising – just as he'd said it would – and the helm hardening, yet I never presumed to suggest putting a reef in. I didn't think it was my place; I assumed with all that insight he'd make the call at the right moment. It never happened.

We needed to be close-hauled to clear shallows, yet we were having to ease the main in big dollops to prevent the boat from

rounding up into the wind; the result is we were further off the wind than we'd be if we had reefed down. Eventually we just about managed to claw our way into Felixstowe and in the dark, in the entrance to the harbour, we wrestled the sails down and motored in towards the River Orwell. With the wind on the nose, the bow kept blowing off the wind even on full power. I don't know what strength the wind was but I call that a force to be reckoned with. Eventually, after half a dozen attempts had been foiled by the wind, we picked up a buoy further up the Orwell.

It was a restless night and I suspect I talked in my troubled sleep, babbling – or maybe even praying – in half-remembered snatches of Latin, 'Oh toyotalexus, nimbostratus, blinkinridiculus, Amen!'

In the morning, the skipper looked skyward and resumed his high-mass weather prediction service. I decided to give him a bit of my own weather lore and, squinting at the heavens, intoned, 'It's an ill dog that blows no wind.' I still don't think he's figured that one out.

LESSON**S**<del> </del>**NOT** LEARNED

Stay indoors. Weather happens outdoors.

YOU'RE BARKING

IF YOU THINK BOATING WITH DOGS IS FUN

BART! LEAVE!!

I'm no great authority on genetic engineering but I'm fairly certain that if you crossed a seal with an RYA Yachtmaster you'd end up with something very closely resembling a Labrador; for surely few other breeds are so sea-kindly.

Unfortunately, my dog Bart is a Jack Russell terrier, which basically means he's a randy criminal mastermind with severe Attention Deficit Hyperactivity Disorder. And the sad truth is that while I go sailing to relax, he has his own agenda. He thinks my boat is just a longer-lasting dog chew.

There's a couple at Stone Sailing Club on the River Blackwater who sail a Wayfarer and a Hunter 19 with a pair of beautifully behaved placid black Labradors. I've often watched with envy

that extraordinary bond of co-operation, loyalty and mutual respect between dog and human. The four are a single unit: one fetches the oars, the other inflates the tender and the Labradors break out a flask of tea and trade sections of the *Daily Telegraph*. To be fair, some weekends it's the other way round.

Then I turn my head and watch Bart roll in something dead, dab it liberally behind each ear, then strut proudly up and down the foreshore, giving off the aroma of eau de dead seagull. To him it's an exclusive aftershave that makes him a guaranteed bitch magnet.

Once I've caught him and cleaned him I wrestle him into his Day-Glo buoyancy aid, which I think not only is sensible but also looks pretty cute. However, he regards it as not only a slur on his manhood but also a sartorial abomination. As I row out to my boat, instead of standing proudly in the bow of my tender, like those noble Yachtmaster Labradors, he's thrashing around in the bottom eating the buoyancy aid off his back.

Often by the time we get to the boat he's hobbled himself by somehow managing to get two legs stuck through one leghole. This makes him angry. Once aboard I try to settle him in one corner of the cockpit, and I've come to accept that the price for his grudging compliance is to allow him to gnaw through the gel-coat, so that most of the smooth edges on my boat now resemble Wensleydale.

If at all possible, I try to sail off my mooring, not in an effort to be flash, but simply to keep the peace. Bart's greatest hate in life is motorbikes, and whenever I start my outboard he stops eating my boat and attempts to savage the engine. Some people use microdots to protect their outboards from theft, but if ever mine gets stolen, I'll just give the police a dental impression of Bart's bite taken from cockpit coaming.

Many sailors on the Blackwater consider jetskis a nuisance, if not a downright hazard, and Bart, for once, is of a similar mind. On several occasions I've caught him in mid-leap as he attempted to launch himself at a passing jetskier. To my shame I must admit I don't always show wholehearted disapproval, but my greatest fear is that one day he'll bury his fangs in the neoprene rump of a passing waterskier and be whisked off at 20 knots across the bay – with a wide-eyed, manic grin and his ears flapping in the wind. I just know this would be Bart's idea of fun.

And with Bart, the fun never ends. Once back ashore as the Labradors dutifully deflate the tender and flush their outboard, Bart will be off after lady-fenders. At least in this department he shows a little discrimination, because when it comes to romance he's interested in humping only fenders with those nice furry fender-socks.

God knows what deranged mutant creature their offspring would be!

LESSONS NOT LEARNED

Sell the Jack Russell.

THE KEEL ISSUE

(WARNING: THIS ONE'S A BIT PRACTICAL, BUT IT WON'T HELP. SORRY.)

'Ah... I see you have a touch of electrolysis...'

This season has not gone according to plan. Not that there's actually been a plan, as such, but I did imagine that by now I would have resumed my own particular brand of bump-and-whooaah east-coast flailing.

Instead, my Sailfish trailer-sailer is still in my back yard in London – and in some ways it's just as well. This past winter was the first time I've overwintered my own boat and I really got it all wrong. I'd read enough of *PBO* consultant sage Andrew Simpson's erudite work to know that I should have made a list or something with a particular kind of pencil which, if it fell into the bilge, would not cause some biblical chemical reaction that would instantly turn every nut, bolt, screw and fitting to powder. The trouble was that it was a bit too chilly and wet to actually go outside and

clamber all over the whole 18-and-a-half foot length of *Marlin*; so instead I cosied up with magazines, charts and books. To fuel dreams of sailing in the high latitudes and walking among the Inuit tribes of Lowestoft I read Janet Harber's *East Coast Rivers*; to prepare myself for that all-too-easy navigational cock-up there was Moitessier's *Cape Horn: The Logical Route*; for a glimpse into a world of impossible glamour and unfeasible slacks there was *Yachting Monthly*; and to make me really worried about things breaking there was *PBO*.

Suddenly it was April and my cunning for avoidance was running out. There was an issue I knew I had to address: the keel. The Sailfish's vertically lifting keel (a GRP wing shape with 250lb of lead in the bottom) is both a virtue and a vice. Its chief virtue is that winding it up on its screw reduces draft from 3ft to 1ft and allows you to probe into creeks and dry out. However, one drawback is that it can fall off if the nut at the bottom of the screw winds itself off, causing noticeably more leeway.

Before the beginning of last season I carried out the recommended modification and fitted a retaining strap to the top of the keel. To be extra sure, I also threaded some copper wire through the hollow pin in the stainless-steel nut at the bottom of the screw, twisted it tight and added a blob of Araldite – just to be sure, to be sure, to be sure.

Since then Andrew Simpson's words have been eating into my mind. I remember reading something about the terrors of electrolytic corrosion caused when different metals mix with seawater, and I was worried. I lifted the screw and found the bottom nut and copper tie perfectly intact (I've since removed the copper tie), but there was something else that wasn't right; the keel was at least half full of primordial Essex goo. I noticed the top of the trailing edge was badly chipped and realised I'd have to lift the keel up through its slot into the cabin to investigate.

This involved a Heath Robinson arrangement of bottle jacks, chocks and blocks, levers and ratchet straps, murderous rage, suicidal desperation and tears; the great pyramids at Giza were built with less sweat.

The rear vertical edge of the keel had a jagged split for most of its length, caused I'm pretty certain by the mooring chain wrapping round the keel and rasping it away like a cheese grater on a thin wedge of Parmesan. I think I've effected a repair that will get me through the season.

I should thank Andrew too, for while I generally find that any new knowledge just creates new worry, if I hadn't been worried about the keel nut I wouldn't have noticed the gaping hole in my keel. On the other hand, while I knew nothing of the gaping hole I wasn't worried. It's a delicate balance, this sailing lark, so next winter, as well as *PBO*, perhaps I should also read a novel that makes no mention of anything remotely watery or boaty – a Harry Potter, for example. Anything else will just make me worry.

LESSONS ~~NOT~~ LEARNED

A little knowledge is a dangerous thing. Try to avoid it

THE LONESOME TRAIL

'Very impressive emergency stop, Sir!'

I'll be honest, sailing terrifies me. I'm not talking about a wrong-way single-handed coracle crossing of the Southern Ocean; I just mean sailing in general.

But there's one thing that scares me even more and that's the truly petrifying prospect of trailering a boat. It's become pretty clear to me during my short time afloat that no one really knows very much about sailing; and as for trailering, no one knows anything at all. Ask owners of exactly the same boat and trailer as you, and one will insist upon minimum tyre pressures of 50psi (that's 55psi magnetic, not true), while another will tell you it's against the law to inflate tyres beyond 22.75psi (but during British Summer Time you must add 1psi). With tombstone gravity, both will separately warn you of the apocalyptic consequences of ignoring their advice – or heeding anyone else's. So what do you do?

I thought I had a cunning plan. My mooring on the Blackwater is a 60-mile white-knuckle tow from my East London home. On the other hand, the Thames is just 10 minutes from my doorstep. So what I thought I'd do was launch on the Thames, berth for a bit in a London marina and make a holiday of sailing back to my east-coast mooring. The problem was that launching at one of the few marinas that had lifting-in facilities wasn't going to leave much change from £100, and when your boat is as modest as my 18-foot Sailfish any expenditure beyond the price of a sponge and bucket represents a considerable proportion of the boat's overall value.

I considered several much cheaper cash proposals from cockney bar-stool matelots who offered a low-tech launch based on optimum levels of alcohol and the combined impetus of several pairs of Doc Marten boots. They all swore they'd done it loads of times, although they were a bit evasive about the insurance side of things.

But on the Thames there's an even cheaper option. You can launch free on public slipways. I inspected several downriver from Tower Bridge and it was while contemplating the solid, menacing mass of inky river sucking past the slimy, darkly glistening slipway at North Woolwich that I came to another conclusion: that while sailing in general and trailering are merely petrifying, the prospect of slipping my boat into the Thames scared me stiffer than Ellen MacArthur's old oilies.

It seemed options were running out, until just round the next bend in the river I found Gallions Point Marina at the eastern end of the Victoria and Albert Docks. It's not exactly what many south-coast sailors would recognise as a marina; there's no David Lloyd leisure centre, no terraced bar, in fact no terrace, no bar, and no yacht club. What it did have, though, was the solution to my problem; for a mere 40 quid they would put my boat in

the water using a monster forklift truck. Perfect. With strops led under my boat from the prongs, Brian and Keith tenderly lifted my little 1000lb minnow of a boat and left it suspended at a convenient height, so I could finish the anti-fouling while they had lunch. After lunch they lowered her gently into the dock and held her on the strops until I'd made sure there were no leaks. It was stress-free and effortless.

The immediate plan is to nudge out into the Thames on little trips and day sails. Seven miles upriver, right by Tower Bridge and the Tower of London, is picturesque St Katharine's dock. One night for two at the Tower Thistle hotel would cost about £160; a night on board *Marlin* would cost £22. That's what I call value.

Further ahead, I'll tiptoe downriver, and if I feel confident enough I just might sail the 90 miles to my mooring on the Blackwater. Failing that, I'll trailer the boat back. Either way, it's bound to be terrifying.

LESSONS ~~NOT~~ LEARNED

Towing a boat is terrifying; sailing is more terrifying. Take up golf.

THE BEST OF
(~~SHIP~~)MATES

We communicated and got along better than at any time.

You could drive from Gallions Point to St Katharine's dock in about 20 minutes. In nautical terms this little jaunt up the Thames to the foot of Tower Bridge is inconsequential, a mere 10 miles or so. But in the shrunken universe of my 18-foot Sailfish it's what I'd definitely call a passage, if not a downright voyage.

Certainly, I'd formed a passage plan of kinds. My partner on this foolhardy venture was Martha, my ex-girlfriend, and the main part of the plan was not to kill each other – either by accident or with intention. For once I felt I actually had the upper hand, because while my sailing experience is pretty rudimentary, hers was nil. This meant, for once, she would have to not only actually listen to me – unprecedented – but also trust me and rely on me – even more unprecedented. It was almost worth it just for the resentment it would create in her; unfortunately, that was matched by my own sense of dark foreboding. Perhaps I should have postponed sailing with Martha until I'd bought a catamaran

with quick-release hulls, so we could just split everything down the middle and go our separate ways.

When I go sailing I normally inform people when I expect to be back. This time, with Martha on board, I felt I needed a little extra insurance and started shouting out my details to pedestrians whenever I stopped at traffic lights on the way to the marina. I explained to Martha that this was standard nautical procedure.

At the marina I familiarised Martha with the boat, which with a Sailfish basically involves pointing and saying, 'There it is.' We ran through emergency numbers and the VHF and sorted out the lifejackets. Martha was unfairly suspicious that hers was an evilly contrived non-floating type, so I swapped it for one she thought would explode.

Our first real test of teamwork was locking out on to the Thames. The power is quite terrifying and we felt like a pea being tossed around in a slimy kitchen sink as huge forces try to suck it down the plug hole.

But we got through it and as our Mariner 3.3hp put-putted us out into the mighty Thames, I think we both realised something: we both needed each other. I couldn't sail the boat without her, and neither could she without me. Nominally, I suppose I was the skipper, but really a relationship on board is one of complete mutual dependency; you have to communicate clearly, listen and respect one another. This master–servant attitude I've seen from so many recreational skippers, especially towards women, is rubbish.

Martha helmed as I raised the sails and we got the little faded blue tub sailing as well as I've known her to. Perhaps having to explain things clearly also helped me understand things better. For some reason, we chatted in near whispers, as we wafted up the river on a benign breeze. Perhaps we felt humbled by Old

Father Thames, touched by its course through history and the thought of those souls who had sailed this way before, through 2000 years and more, as the river gave birth to and succoured this great city. It felt good to feel small.

We felt proud, too, as we locked into St Katharine's dock by the Tower of London; we were little bigger than the tenders on most of the other boats alongside in the lock – and that was a source of pride. We'd achieved something and we couldn't resist letting people know.

As we gorged ravenously at the picturesque Dickens Inn overlooking the dock, we hoped strangers overheard us say 'our boat' now and then. Later she became 'our yacht' and we didn't mind at all if, when we gestured vaguely towards the boats, people assumed ours was the classic 65-foot ketch, rather than the minnow cosily tucked in behind it and completely out of sight, except for the very top of her gently jiggling mast.

Anyone who's been around boats has seen sailing couples fall out and relationships founder. But for me and Martha it seemed we communicated and got along better than at any time. Sadly, though, we know our time has been, and as we lay in our berths and gazed up into the night, watching the mast touch each star in turn and, like a magic wand, command them to twinkle, just for old times' sake – we had a blazing row!

LESSONS NOT LEARNED

Sailing with ex-girlfriends is more terrifying than towing.
(I don't get it – why have I got so many ex-girlfriends?)

HOW NOT TO LAUNCH A BOAT

'I wonder if I might make a suggestion...'

My friends Julian and Ted are what you'd call very, very experienced sailors. Ted, who is the more senior, took his Yachtmaster practical exam in a reed boat, while Julian didn't really start sailing until the end of the last Ice Age. Apparently, neither of them rates Noah very highly.

Anyway, while I usually have to resort to subterfuge, lies and deceit to get anyone on, or even near, my boat, Ted and Julian are a little more doughty than most. Just say to them, 'Do you fancy spending a day getting really cold, wet, filthy, bloody, bruised and grazed?' and they'll say, 'Ooh, yes please.' I'd even told them that we weren't actually going sailing – and they were still keen. The plan was to trailer my boat from London and plonk it in on its mooring on the beautiful Blackwater estuary in Essex. Foolishly I

thought I'd kind of be the skipper for the launch day and they'd be crew, but the moment they arrived at my house I began to have the feeling that I was being 'taken in hand' as part of some kind of nautical care-in-the-community project.

It was clear the two of them had been colluding at length, but when I asked Julian why he was bringing along a length of rope long enough to lead to the centre of Hampton Court maze, and back he was evasive almost to the point of being shifty and just muttered vaguely, 'Oh, it might come in handy for something.'

Once on the hard at Stone Sailing Club, each time I made an attempt to take charge the devious duo asked for a cup of tea. When I returned with the first round of tea I noticed the rope had reappeared in a huge coil beside the boat. Some time later, with every single cup in the sailing club lined up on the sea wall with cold un-drunk tea, they'd raised the mast, rigged the entire boat, mounted the outboard, inflated the tender and made an elegant zigzag pattern with the rope by the water's edge. I wasn't even going to give the rotten pair of plotters the satisfaction of asking what it was doing there, 'cos they'd just mutter something vague like 'Oh, it makes a rather nice pattern, don't you think,' or 'It's drying' – and then flash sly conspiratorial glances at each other.

I needed to take control and so I told them – quite firmly – how we'd go about launching the boat. We'd dunk the whole lot in the water, flail around a bit, fill our Wellington boots, then discard them, get wet at least to the neck, panic, flail around a bit more, try to catch the boat as it floats away, desperately tug at the outboard starter while we either blow onshore or career off to hit the most beautiful little wooden gaffer you've ever seen and whose owner is aboard applying the 27th coat of varnish.

It's always worked for me in the past!

After flashing another of those evil, smug glances at Ted, Julian simpered, 'I wonder if I might make a small suggestion.' The next thing I know he's rowing off in the tender with one end of the rope, ties it to a scrubbing post way out in the water and connects the other to the stern of my boat. Then, as Ted reversed the trailer progressively into the water, Julian took up the slack of the rope from on board. Gently, totally in control, *Marlin* floated off as Julian pulled her to the scrubbing post. He then led the rope to the bow (so it wouldn't be near the prop) and started the outboard. Then he smarmed, 'Of course, laddie, if we didn't have the scrubbing posts we could have done the same thing with your anchor.'

I was in awe – and in two minds. Clearly he was a smug bastard, but I had to admit he was also a genius. I could have sailed a lifetime and never ever thought of this simple, brilliant trick. What's more, I don't think you'd ever learn it on any practical sailing course, either.

I had to ask him how he'd thought of it. He said, 'Years of sailing small yachts without engines. Now how about a cup of tea, laddie.'

LESSONS NOT LEARNED

Humility, inadequacy, resentment, inferiority.

BACK TO SKOOL

'Oh, do continue, Mr Smith. You were just saying how easy it was…!'

Life's not all about what you know; it's not even about who you know; it's actually all about where you sit. If only someone had told me this the first time I walked trembling into a classroom, by now I'd have at least one 150-foot superyacht and be spending most of my time lounging by the afterdeck jacuzzi in a monogrammed towelling robe. Whenever I got a little restless I'd take a trip to the jacuzzi on the foredeck. That's fulfilment! Instead I've got a Sailfish 18.

It's not the sort of mistake you want to make twice in life, so when I enrolled at the Hardknock Inner City School of Pre-natal Yoga, Safe Cracking and Day Skippery I was determined to sit in the right place. It could be a pivotal moment – life-changing.

Yet, as I stood in the doorway, I froze. Suddenly I was seven again, short-trousered, scab-kneed, in my pockets a pot-pourri

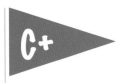

of conkers, congealed sweets and mystery fluff. I trembled and flushed and felt hostile eyes boring into me as I stumbled to my seat. I just about managed to execute my plan: A) sit in the front – that way you're spared the humiliation of the whole class turning round and watching you blush crimson when the teacher asks your name and you say, 'I dunno, can't remember, Sir'; B) avoid the fat bloke; C) sit next to someone who's got a Louis Vuitton briefcase and an impressive array of expensive-looking electronic gadgets on his desk.

I can't really say my plan was wholly successful. Posh Peter on my right had a real Rolex on his wrist, a home on Guernsey, another in London and a catamaran in the British Virgin Islands. On my left was Keith, clearly smart but not too nerdy. The trouble was that Peter turned out to be hugely thick and a bad influence, and Keith wouldn't let me cheat – I mean, borrow his notes. The other flaw in my plan was me – ten minutes back in school and I'd regressed dramatically.

First I started scribbling obscenities on Peter's course books and we quickly progressed to routinely stabbing each other with dividers. It was just a bit of fun, but the humourless sod never invited me on his yacht. As for Keith, he was forever getting top marks in everything, so when we marked our own exercises I'd wait until he read out his marks, then I'd add one per cent and read out mine. As he quite often scored 99.5% I regularly got over 100 – all without ever doing any work.

That was the other problem – I've always been a lousy student, but I was certainly not the worst. In fact, it soon became a matter of pride to exasperate our teacher with our blinding stupidity – and we didn't even have to try. Poor old bearded Brian; he started each class looking like a genial Captain Bird's Eye and ended each evening snorting, throbbing, livid-hued, like an angry Thor on the verge of a coronary. Once, in a session on anchoring, one puzzled

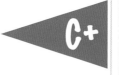

student asked him, 'Isn't a kedge a kind of boat?' Another time, when Brian patiently explained there were two high tides a day, someone asked, 'How many low ones are there?'

But the best moment of mass incomprehension was when Brian used the innocuous term 'floating gin palace'. The trouble was that for many inner-city London students it was just not part of their cultural frame of reference, yet they became convinced that unlocking the secret meaning of the phrase was the key to passing the whole course. If only he'd said 'floating crack house' that might have registered, but with each of his efforts to explain, the chasm of misunderstanding opened wider. After 20 minutes of deepening cross-cultural confusion he blurted out, 'Forget it – there aren't any questions on gin palaces in the exam.'

At the end of it all, most of us managed to scrape through, but the most gratifying thing was that smug, clever Keith didn't come top. That honour fell to a sweet little old lady nurse who had never been on a boat. When Brian asked his star student how she was going to pursue sailing further, she said, 'Oh, I'm not, I just like to do a different course each year.'

LESSONS ~~NOT~~ LEARNED

Umm, I'm sure I learned something but I can't put my finger on it right now. Oh yeah, I remember. Don't become a teacher.

SARTORIAL HORROR

'Sorry, guys, I think I mixed up metric and imperial…'

It's a little-known fact that Halloween is in fact an ancient pagan nautical tradition. At the end of each October when rosy-cheeked kids don scary masks, fangs and capes to go door-to-door trick or treating, there's a far more disturbing ritual being played out on foreshores up and down the land.

It's at this time that sailors are irresistibly drawn – as if by a mysterious supernatural power – to gather where water meets the land in conspiratorial huddles and berobe themselves in hideous sartorial abominations far more terrifying than any Halloween get-up you dare to imagine: gnarled walnut knees on stick-like legs protruding from skimpy, crotch-shaping 1970s polyester football shorts; tattered engineering overalls that Fred Dibnah would have had put down years ago; ragged plimsolls whose emissions have been named and shamed as more toxic than

any other known greenhouse gas under the Kyoto agreement on the environment; neck-high rubber waders that frankly have no place outside the bedroom; and – most terrifying of all – tracksuit bottoms that have entirely eroded away inside a brittle carcass made up of 20 years' deposits of anti-fouling epoxy resin, waterproof grease and bilge paint.

At least that's what the age-old seasonal ritual of 'lifting out' looks like on the east coast. As for the south coast, I'm sure the marina boutiques down there offer several exclusive colour-co-ordinated ranges of high-performance, laying-up and lifting-out designer wear, designed to provide maximum comfort while you guide operations from the yacht-club veranda.

Lifting out is one of those many dark arts of sailing that provide immense amusement for anyone not actually doing it. That's why I try, if I can, to do it when there are as few witnesses as possible. This year I arrived at Stone Sailing Club at 6.30am as the weak wedge of dawn began to lift the curtain of night. By 8.30, working alone and with the stealth of a jewel thief, I had edged my trailer to the edge of the rising tide. As I rowed my tender out to my boat I turned to look shoreward – and suddenly before me there materialised a ghoulish apparition: the entire lifting-out coven, all of them apparelled in their hideous ceremonial garb. Maybe it was a trick of the light, but I'd swear they'd erected a grandstand complete with smoked-glass corporate hospitality suite, ticket turnstiles and a burger concession.

With the keel raised, the handling of my Sailfish is slightly on the nervous side of skittish and it caused great merriment as I swerved and scudded back and forth past my trailer like a hopeless kamikaze moth failing to do itself in on a light bulb. But the moment I came within reach, the lift-out squad scooped me up and in a single, neat seamless move had me high, dry and safe on the hard, my boat perfectly centred on its trailer.

While I prepared my boat for trailering home I had time to wonder at their sorcery as they landed boat after boat with not a scratch to man, woman or boat.

For once I saw bilge keelers really come into their own as their owners simply rammed the shore Normandy-landing-style and waited for the sea to go away (then once back on terra firma I'm told they can be fitted with castor wheels and converted into passable dodgems, but without the windward capability). Meanwhile, to provide the bilge keelers with a little entertainment there was a deep-draughted racy fin-keeler out in the deeper water trying to locate its cradle somewhere below in the murky depths. The crew had attached a lattice of long vertical bamboo canes which poked out of the water from the cradle below. The canes had bands of coloured tape on them which obviously meant something. Foreshore opinion was divided as to whether the strange trellis was part of a Day Skipper practical exam, an Indonesian fish trap, or a pagan offering – along the lines of the Wicker Man. In any case, once they'd scattered the canes they seemed to find it easier to settle, more or less, on their cradle.

Even if Wallace and Gromit went yachting on Halloween in a Carry On movie spectacular I doubt they'd be able to rival 'lifting out' as the most enjoyable nautical spectacle ever invented.

LESSONS NOT LEARNED

Arrive early, bring a camcorder, send the footage to You've Been Framed, use the £200 fee to pay someone to lift your boat out. That's an Impractical Boat Owner tip-top, top-notch, top-drawer tip.

FLUSHED WITH PRIDE

'So, how badly do you need to go?'

I don't want to make owners of lesser Sunseekers feel any more inadequate than strictly necessary, but my Sailfish must surely be the only 18½-footer in the world with two toilets.

This gives me considerable advantages, not just in the corporate hospitality market but also socially. I recall with pride one particular weekend last summer when my friend Angie timidly enquired about my on-board facilities. I'd remembered well the lessons from my total leadership seminar at a Travelodge near Swindon (£49.50 including eat-as-much-as-you-like buffet lunch) where our mentoring facilitator had told us, 'Give the punters choice.'

He would have been flushed with pride to see me dive below, re-emerge brandishing two brand-new toilets, one in each hand, and with casual sophistication offer Angie the choice of 'One litre or two?' I felt so suave that if I'd been wearing a tuxedo I'd have been tempted to say, 'Shaken or stirred?' And Angie clearly was ... shaken and stirred. I could also tell by the expression on her

face – slightly pained – that she was giving weighty consideration to her options.

Now, the more finicky among you might point out that the correct skippery term for toilet is 'heads', but you'd be wrong. The actual correct nautical term for my Sailfish toilets is 'jugs' and I've got to tell you they were exceptional value. I got a nest of three plastic jugs for a quid – and you just can't argue with that, although I suppose the half-litre one is a bit more ornamental than strictly practical.

There have been times I've envied Ellen MacArthur her sponsorship from B&Q, but if I'm honest pretty much everything they offer is far too exotic for my humble cruising-oriented chandlery needs. However, if a chain of pound shops offered to sponsor me I'd leap at the chance. In fact, they wouldn't even have to sponsor me – just a quid off everything would be fine. But even paying full price, I just can't pass a pound shop without buying something vital for my boat.

Pound-shop tools are a good buy. They may be bendy and rust instantly, but as you're never going to use them what does it matter? And when they plop over the side you've lost only a quid – or, looked at differently, you've saved about 70 quid compared with a titanium self-harming multi-tool tested in the Southern Ocean (where it still sinks). On my boat the interior is festooned with pound-shop lights, powered by pound-shop batteries, which means the ambience starts to become seductively dim about 10 seconds after you've installed a new battery. Along each side of the boat in the bow I've got very colourful fabric nursery storage pouches designed for dolls, teddies and toys, and also invaluable for stowing other pound-shop essentials. All my plates, bowls, knives, forks, spoons, hooks, pegs and buckets are pound shop, but even more than anything else the interior of my boat is a mad pile-'em-high bazaar of Day-Glo plastic containers.

They are all vital. For example, apart from the ones that contain 'stuff', others contain other containers, and some just fit perfectly. An unexpected bonus of all these sealed containers is that if my boat had any more positive buoyancy it would in fact become lighter than air.

But you can't get all your sailing needs from pound shops. More recently I've broadened my horizons and have started scanning those 'bright idea' and 'outdoorsy type' mail order catalogues you get with the Sunday supplements. Of course, the gear is that much more costly, but what price safety? I'm thinking hard about the £14.99 full-length non-slip bath mat (aka cockpit sole mat) and the battery-operated intruder alert that barks like an Alsatian, but I'm not sure a burglar would believe my boat had a resident guard dog that big on board – if they did a chihuahua version I'd definitely go for that. In one of the catalogues I even saw a compact chemical toilet, but that's a preposterous notion – I'd never displace my pound-shop treasures for such a frivolous gimmick.

LESSONS NOT LEARNED

This gave me a bit of a 'heads up' as most of my female friendships went down the pan when I bought my Sailfish. Fact is women are a little bit fussy. Apart from Ellen MacArthur, Naomi James and Clare Francis, they don't really seem to like boats unless they're tied up to a pontoon in Monte Carlo. The trouble with that is that you then get stiletto-heel punctures all over your Sailfish. Basically, if you own a Sailfish, sail with blokes. You haven't got any choice.

A LUVVERLY PAIR OF LOCKERS

*'Sir, you've been admiring our engine bay for a while now.
Is there anything we can help you with?'*

'Yes – could you please call a chiropractor…?'

There was a time when Boat Show yacht salesmen used to terrify me.

It was not so long ago in my leprous outcast years as a boatless wannabe that I looked on them as vengeful authority figures, ranking right up there with God, social workers and nightclub bouncers. And even earlier than that, in my hormonally charged youth, I'd quickly learned that these kipper-tied, polyester playboys lived for one reason only; namely to keep me off their boats – and, believe me, I knew it was personal.

Of course, looking back from my mature plateau of hormone serenity, I now realise they're only there to stop you nicking the vases. Even so, it's been a long, hard learning process. I remember my early Earl's Court years, when I was aching to look inside any yacht at all; it took me years to pluck up the courage to run the gauntlet of the terrifying front-desk Rottweilers with lip gloss.

Then one year, somehow, all of a sudden, hyperventilating and my pores gushing like a fire sprinkler, I was inside a boat for the first time (ahhh, I'll never forget that first heady whiff of glassfibre, solvents, releasing agents and glue). 'Look normal, look normal, look normal' was the panic-stricken mantra I repeated silently to myself as my thudding heart tried to force my eyeballs out of my head. How embarrassing if my eyes popped out and rolled around the cabin sole, then disappeared into the bilges. Still, that would be one way of avoiding the salesman's piercing gaze. The other way was to repeatedly open and close a locker door as if I was completely absorbed in assessing the lightness of the action, firmness of the latch and smoothness of the hinges. It didn't work.

'What do you sail?' he asked. My shower-head setting shot from cascade to full Niagara mode; my heart thumped so violently the boat began to shift on its cradle. If it fell off I'd have to pay for it. Think, panic, think, how could I say 'Nothing'? – it would be too humiliating. Panic, think, panic. 'Lovely lockers,' I said in an involuntary spasm. Then, I simply ceased to exist and all at once became calm – a bit like drowning.

But I didn't die and I've come a long way since then. I quickly learned to have a catalogue of boat names at the ready, so that when asked that killer question I now just mention a yacht that's slightly shorter than the one I'm on. This generally gets them interested and next they delicately enquire, 'How would you like to fund the purchase?' Usually, to keep it simple, I just say, 'Oh, cash probably.' The reason I say 'probably' is that some of the yacht reps would actually prefer to sell you a finance package that earns them commission – I like to give them a bit of encouragement.

Over the years I've refined my techniques and I've managed to have a good nose around most of the biggest yachts at shows – and have a bit of harmless fun. If I'm on anything over 60 feet long I'll ask whether there's a bilge-keel version, which of course

there isn't. 'Oh, that's a shame,' I say as I hand back the brochure and saunter off. And if I'm on the biggest yacht a company has ever made, I generally ask, 'Haven't you got anything bigger?'

My crowning moment was when I was on a superyacht. I calmly asked the price – it was millions, pounds not euros! – then enquired whether that included fenders and warps. And you know what, the salesman actually went off to find out. Or maybe he was fetching security. I'll never know – I left before he returned.

A while ago I briefed a non-yachting friend on how to deal with the killer question and, for sheer devilment, told him to say his family had outgrown their Laser Pico (a one-man dinghy the size of an espadrille). Amazingly, no one batted an eyelid.

Then it came to me, in a blinding flash. Those guys inside the big flash yachts, they're not all salesmen: half of them are security, hired in to make sure you don't start unscrewing fittings. You could say you sailed a Narcissist 666 or a Necromancer Harbinger of Doom for all that it matters. In fact you could even tell them you own a Sailfish 18!

LESSONS NOT LEARNED

Nowhere is out of bounds. However, if you're lacking in front and hobbled by honesty and you still really want carte-blanche entrée to the top deck of the boat show canapé circuit, nothing works better than casually flourishing a Sunseeker brochure; you can usually find one discarded in the Guinness bar if you hang around long enough. It's the VIP passport that gives access all areas, and with it in your hand you'll find the world is your Oyster, Princess, Hallberg Rassy or Swan.

I NEVER INTENDED TO GO SINGLE-HANDED

With each tack the maelstrom of malevolence was unleashed and, if anything, intensified.

I'm convinced that one of the keys to truly heroic single-handed sailing is to do it by yourself. Chichester, Knox-Johnston, MacArthur – I doubt that their lone exploits would be so celebrated if they'd had company. It would somehow diminish their achievements if, when they stepped unsteadily ashore followed by a small posse they'd said, 'Yeah but, no but, they didn't help, honest.'

To me, single-handed sailing represents the pinnacle of human endeavour, so you can imagine how proud I am to join this exalted bunch, although I never actually intended it to happen. Last summer I set off with Martha, my non-sailing ex-partner – I've got quite a few ex-sailing ex-partners as well – on a short

weekend cruise to Heybridge Basin on the north side of the River Blackwater. It's a magical spot and it was supposed to be an idyll. Unfortunately we brought Bart, our Jack Russell terrier, who is not merely dysfunctional and the product of a broken home, but also dyslexic. Naturally when I mentioned 'idyll' he assumed I meant 'ordeal'.

As we let go my mooring at Stone Sailing Club I was full of the kind of dark foreboding you'd get before taking a shower at the Bates Motel. As we wafted upriver on the tide, the light wind aft of the beam gently plumped up our sails to bask in downy fullness under the sun, and the rudder played a secret song of whispered sighs and stolen giggles that floated away on laughing ripples to eternity. Yet something wasn't right. Bart was calm – I'd even say serene, if I didn't know better. This could mean only two things: either that a massive dose of Anthrax, big enough to knock out Milton Keynes, had slightly unsettled his tummy; or that the little bastard was up to something.

Locking into Heybridge Basin with Bart is normally a near-death experience but this time he behaved most oddly ... he behaved! I was worried, but once the boat was tied up snugly he quickly reverted to normal and set up his regular exclusion zone of snarling menace around *Marlin*. This also placed the pub, showers and toilets off limits to all other visiting sailors, unless they were prepared to row across the basin and walk the long way round across the lock. All perfectly normal.

To my relief we didn't get barred, and on an outing with Bart that counts as a success. However, next day, as we set off on the return journey I still had that Bates Motel feeling in the pit of my stomach. As we locked out and hoisted sail Bart was calm enough, but keeping a keen eye on things. Then it happened. I called, 'Ready about,' put the tiller down – and all hell broke loose. As the genoa flapped across and the sheets ran free, Bart went

ballistic, jumping up to shred the sail, then wrestling Martha for the sheets as she tried to haul in.

I said to Martha, 'He'll just have to get used to it,' but I was wrong. With each tack the maelstrom of malevolence was unleashed and, if anything, intensified. After half a dozen goes our nerves were in tatters. They say gentlemen never sail to windward, and neither does Bart. The only thing for it was for Martha to take him below (which on a Sailfish is still within snapping distance) and restrain him during tacks. That left me alone up top.

The idea of tacking by myself was terrifying. The first time was a disastrous tangle of confusion as I tried to figure out how to handle the tiller while letting one rope go and pulling in another and keeping a lookout for other boats and not running aground on a falling tide. It was too much to do.

Again and again, I fumbled, flailed and fell about while Martha and the mutt wrestled below. Eventually, though, I started to get it together and managed to go about with a degree of co-ordination. It was a brilliant feeling of accomplishment.

Martha popped her head up from below and said, 'You're really enjoying this, aren't you?' And I really was. I was beaming from ear to ear. Chichester, Knox-Johnston, MacArthur, Selby, I was one of them, a single-hander – well, sort of.

As we sailed to the south of Osea Island more and more boats started to appear. Coming towards me on the opposite tack was a 30-footer. Was I on port tack, starboard tack, which was the stand-on vessel, who should give way? Suddenly my mind was numb. I couldn't think. As the boat loomed larger even Martha and Bart stopped wrestling (Bart may even have whimpered).

I held on, fighting the gigantic impulse to bear away, trying to recall my Day Skipper mantras. Then, the boat dipped under our stern, he waved and I waved back. Relief. I was on starboard. I was the stand-on vessel. I got it right, he got it right too, but I so very nearly panicked.

We tacked across each other a few more times and as we parted for the last time he shouted across, 'You're sailing well.' My whole body tingled with huge pride and my eyes filled up.

Once ashore, I felt as if I'd sailed round the world instead of six miles. I was emotionally drained and physically depleted, and as I headed for the shower I wouldn't even have been bothered if it was in the Bates Motel.

LESSONS NOT LEARNED

Earlier in this book I suggested selling the Jack Russell. That didn't work – there were no takers. The next step is to give the Jack Russell away, and if that fails drive him to westest west wales and drop him off there. If he finds his way home, try to get him featured as Practical Boat Owner's Sea Dog of the Month and mention that he has a lust to round Cape Horn. Someone's bound to lap it up and take him off your hands.

THE MAXIMUM BOAT (IT DOES WHAT IT SAYS ON THE TUB)

'I've done one or two mods, but there's so much more needs doing.'

It's a little-known fact, but one worth knowing, that the quest for perfection is over. In fact it ended a while ago, in 1970 to be precise. But if it escaped your notice it's not your fault, for even today there are fewer than 1000 people in the world who are guardians of this powerful knowledge.

That was the year when a pert blob of petrochemical by-products, otherwise known as the Sailfish 18, made its debut at a Southampton factory – as history recalls – to a fanfare played on a Stylophone, a reception hosted by Miss Gosport (runner-up in the Southampton regional finals) and refreshment provided by endless cans of Party 7 beer. If only the Crimplene-suited PR

man hadn't helped himself so liberally, and if only Miss Gosport hadn't disappeared into the storeroom with the kipper-tied local newspaper man, the event might have made more of a splash.

Even so, there was no denying the virtues – and great value – of this perky piece of rotundity with its wind-up vertically lifting keel. For £848 you got not just the boat, but sails too, a road trailer, a 4hp outboard, anchor, bilge pump, cooker, chemical toilet, cushions, warps, fenders and fire extinguisher; as an extra bonus one of the early boats even came with a pair of hot pants and a Miss Gosport sash stowed under the bunk cushions – whether this was a promotional gimmick or a simple careless oversight is now lost in the mists of time. But either way, what a bargain!

In fact, over the next 20 years or so around 850 Sailfish 18s were built (mine's number 641), and even today they're a pretty common sight round the coast, perched daintily by the receding tide on mounds of sand and mud like cherries on a Mr Kipling tart.

By the misguided conventions of our times some people might describe the Sailfish as a trailer-sailer, but I think the word 'yacht' is more fitting. Early Sailfish publicity boasted of the boat's six-berth accommodation and to my mind that clearly makes it a yacht, although I must say I haven't yet found the other four berths on mine.

That the Sailfish 18 represents the pinnacle of yacht development is pretty much universally agreed – by nearly everyone in the Sailfish Association. In fact some of us have been thinking about commissioning a range of Sailfish-branded sun-strips, T-shirts and stickers emblazoned with the words 'Other yachts are available' and 'It does what it says on the tub'.

The upper echelons of the inner circle of the close-knit Sailfish community have of course been privy to the secret for more than

45 years; but if that powerful knowledge had percolated out into a wider sphere it could have saved Ellen MacArthur a lot of time, money and effort – if only she'd known. Likewise, fellow *PBO* contributor the celebrated novelist Sam Llewellyn has recently discovered the concept of the Minimum Boat. Who'd have thought that more than three decades earlier the Sailfish established the blueprint of the Maximum Boat?

Nevertheless, it's part of the human condition that perfection is never good enough, and in striving beyond perfection Sailfish devotees seem keener than most. The holiest icon of the excellent Sailfish Association is a brilliant tome known as the Modifications Manual, containing 30 years plus of bright ideas, innovations and accumulated wisdom. Obviously, as the lone exemplar of the Maximum Boat the Sailfish has no known faults, merely a series of absorbing idiosyncrasies and entertaining quirks, which are addressed by chapters such as 'Rudders of the falling-off variety', 'Repairing the keel in my cabin' and 'The accessible pump' (surely an improvement on the inaccessible pump).

The subject of raising and lowering the mast has occupied some of the greatest Sailfish thinkers of this and the last century. My, as yet unrefined, method for raising the mast is to con my old-timer pals Julian and Ted into 'a day out' and then hijack a scout troop and any passers-by. Between the 23 of us we normally get it up eventually. The trouble is if you use the same method to lower the mast while on the water, the boat becomes a bit tippy – unless you jettison some of the scouts. That's my way, but various Sailfish gurus have devised really ingenious mechanisms that reduce mast management to a one-person operation, using guys, blocks, poles and something called geometry.

The manual also describes several methods of replacing windows, but I've developed my own way, which was to replace my old leaky ones with new ones that leak in exactly the same places.

The imagination of the Sailfish community is boundless. I've seen a Sailfish with a retracting bowsprit and spinnaker, another with a solar panels, several with real sliding curtains, one with a miniature autopilot and some with more electrical fittings than Dixons. I've even heard tell of one that's been converted to a ketch – really.

With this incredible spirit of innovation it's a wonder to me that a Sailfish owner didn't invent the Sinclair C5 at least 15 years before Sir Clive.

LESSONS **NOT** LEARNED

Purely by accident I bought a great little boat. And one of the best things about it is the fabulous Sailfish Association. In fact, that's a real, genuine, sincere top tip: if you buy a boat with a great association behind it, you'll have a wealth of knowledge, encouragement and kinship to get the best from your boat.

A LITTLE LIGHT DISPLACEMENT

'Clanking noise? Oh, it's probably just the engine…'

Sailing is basically a displacement activity – just ask any RYA instructor, or life coach. However, I have noticed differences in their interpretations. When your RYA instructor tells you about displacement it's a matter of straightforward unfathomable physics – you're not expected to understand it, but simply to memorise it well enough to pass the test. No worries.

When your personal life coach mentions the word, there's no test but it costs more. What they say is that basically everything you have ever done or will do is a displacement activity, a diversion to avoid what you really ought to be doing. Too right. Whenever it's warm and sunny I like to go sailing as often as possible – to avoid work as often as possible. But there are displacement opportunities all year round and the fitting-out month of March

is one of the best times to put theory into practice. It's traditional for sailors to spend most of March suffering as much as possible for pleasures to come. The need for pain is so overwhelming that I'm surprised leading brands of anti-fouling don't come with a free hair shirt, a cheese grater to skin your knuckles and instructions not to apply in winds below force 8.

One of my favourite seasonal displacement activities – apart from looking at pictures of beach barbecues in Sunsail brochures and going to boat jumbles and buying stuff I already got the year before – is the Frost Bite Race on the Thames organised by the Cruising Association. While my boat is lying displaced and untouched in my back yard I normally crew for my bespoke pal Julian on his very posh Rustler 36. I really am no racer (just mention the word spinnaker and I'll go below and bake scones) but for Julian it's a displacement activity, allowing him to shout at me, instead of someone else – for 17 miles, from Limehouse to Erith, and all the way back the following morning.

This year, though, I got the opportunity to take my seasonal displacement to a higher level – 30 tons, to be precise – aboard *Margaret Hamilton*, a pre-war Scottish-built 54-foot wooden MFV owned by Christine Parkinson. Aboard with her husband Neil and old friend Ted, as we chugged downriver to serve as the finish-line boat at Erith, I savoured the solid Mrs Doubtfire curves of this cuddly governess whose racy fire-engine-red topside petticoats brushed the Thames aside – but most of all I relished the warmth of the wheel house.

While the Frost Bite racers grazed raw knuckles on the burning icy metal winches and fumbled numb-handed with lines, we sipped hot soup, stripped to T-shirts and occasionally popped out on deck to cool off. At Erith as we prepared to set the anchor, the flakes of chain snagged and by the time the anchor hit bottom we'd drifted downstream of the finish-line position, with less

depth under us than comfortable on a falling tide. No worries – just reset the anchor.

But try as we might we just couldn't winch the anchor up, so we motored forward a little to slacken the chain, then … thunk! Silence. No engine noise. The buoyed anchor tripping line, the deployment of which had been a matter of earlier debate, had wrapped round the prop and Neil had very quick-wittedly and instantly cut the engine before any serious damage.

Slowly, serenely, we were completely out of control, adrift. A nearby RIB, whose crew were on an RYA powerboat course, came to our aid and alerted Erith Yacht Club's workboat, which strained to tow us across to the south side of the river on to a buoy.

Here was the problem: the anchor was somewhere under the boat; possibly, as the tide turned, the anchor chain could wrap round the buoy's chain; also, if we were taken inshore to a drying mooring we could settle on the anchor and hole the hull. Bad.

We had to find out what was going on underneath, and in the fading light with the immense help of John in the club's trot boat we lifted the chain over the side, link by link, until the anchor emerged, along with the over-spec ¾-inch tripping line attached to the prop.

We recovered the anchor and cut the line. Later, the Erith Yacht Club workboat towed us to an inshore buoy and the next I remember is rolling across the boat, out of control in my sleeping bag at FOUR in the morning, as we settled on the mud. Later, with our tender lying on the mud at the stern we pitched a ladder over the side into it (we were lucky that *Margaret Hamilton's* tool box had a full-size builder's ladder) and Neil went to work on the rope with my prized sailing knife.

It must have taken half an hour to cut through the tight fist of rope round the prop – and then it was time for bacon butties as we waited for the tide to fill. Still aground and at a jaunty angle we watched the Frost Bite racers jostle for the start. An hour or so later we floated off, fired up the engine and trailed the pack back to Limehouse. Later, at the Cruising Association's headquarters

LESSONS NOT LEARNED

Anchors are decorative items and while it's OK to talk about them in shore-based RYA theory courses, they are not really suited to marine applications (much like varnish – and boats, come to think of it). That's why marinas exist, and this is where they have some practical purpose, as the sight of your glinting battering ram heading for a row of parked boats ensures there's always someone on hand to take your lines. If you must use them at sea, best practice, as advised by organisations like the RYA (but not the RYA), is to first unshackle the anchor from its chain, then chuck the anchor overboard, and tie up to a buoy. Not only is this relatively stress-free; you get to keep the chain which

we got a tankard, for what I'm not quite sure, perhaps for being the first finishing boat not to finish the Frost Bite Race. As usual, Greenwich Yacht Club won everything that mattered, but the real heroes were all the brilliant people at Erith Yacht Club who took a potentially very serious crisis and turned it into an anecdote. Thanks, guys.

you can then use to create a decorative nautically themed border for your garden rockery. It also eliminates the possibility of fouling your prop. Come to think of it, you could always buy another anchor to serve as a patio centrepiece, where the gentle patina of rust will, over time, give your garden a mature and romantic feel, instead of staining your deck, anchor locker and bilges.

The only method of anchoring approved by organisations such as the RYA – but not the RYA – is to tie up to a newly-wed couple on a larger boat already at anchor. There's no worry that they'll leave before you because their tripping line will be wrapped round their prop. As they're on their honeymoon they probably want to be left alone, so I'd leave it a week or two before you notify the authorities.

BLIGH AND CHRISTIAN – I CAN SEE BOTH SIDES

'It's been a rough trip, so be careful with… Ah, never mind.'

Not so long ago, when I was a mere crew, a low-born invertebrate, bilge-feeding crustacean in the evolutionary pecking order of yachting, I used to think that the word 'lager' was a proper nautical term.

I'd already learned that every now and then at random intervals when no one's expecting it you're supposed to shout things like 'Eeyore' and 'Ready avast'. And through careful study of yachts coming alongside pontoons I'd quickly grasped that once you've tossed a slipknot over a mooring cleat, all the crew are supposed to beat their chests, throw their heads back, shout 'Lager' in unison and then sprint off down the pontoon. With some of the

racing crews you can't help but wonder at the slickness of the teamwork. Then, as you reach the shore, someone – normally the most sensitive one – is supposed to call back, 'Oy, skipper, do you want anything from the shops?' The important thing here is to be sure you're out of earshot.

Ah, happy days! How things have changed. Back then, as we settled in for the night around a mound of steaming Mustos, one of the main topics of our loud-mouthed inebriate bar-room chatter was how stressed and anti-social skippers always are. Tight, too. Strange how most skippers always seem to bowl in just after the barman's called time – more than just coincidence, don't you think? And the ones who actually deign to arrive before last orders just stand there strobing and occulting like a quick-flashing port-hand mark when they ought to be at the bar buying a round. Some of them really seem to have no idea of team spirit.

How blissful ignorance was. That was all of two years ago. Now I'm older and wiser, I've bought a boat and I've done some courses and even got a 'stifficate' or two. I've also come to understand a fundamental yachting truth: that there must be a rift of mutual resentment between skipper and crew – it's simply the way of the sea.

When I bought my boat, I was determined not to be one of those uptight skippers, always stressing about things and critically scrutinising every movement, breath and muscle tick of anyone who stepped aboard my domain.

But the trouble is that crew just don't understand the momentous responsibility that weighs upon the shoulders of us skippers. While they're playing with iPods, texting pals, poring over pub guides and threatening mutiny if you don't set a course for a quayside pub run by their favourite brewery, we'll be churning over slightly more weighty matters, like tides, currents, winds, trying to figure out where the hell we are and generally not killing anyone.

And that's not even the half of it. For days before we set off I'll have been fretting about weather systems, downloading synoptic charts off the web, pounding premium-rate fax lines and printing off enough paisley swirls to wallpaper your local Tandoori. None of it makes much sense to me but it helps me feel I'm taking my responsibilities seriously. Then I'll get a call enquiring about how sunny it's going to be and what factor sunblock to bring! Don't they know I've got more important things on my mind? Have we got enough fuel? What's that creaking sound? Is the rig going to collapse? Will the sails rip? Will every rope, sheet and line unravel or part? Will the keel fall off?

Crew, however, seem mostly to have one major concern, and that's 'Where are the ginger nuts?' And you should see the sloppy way they eat them – if those crumbs get into the bilge, who knows what the possible consequences could be? In fact, there's only one question that annoys me more, and that is 'When are we going to get there?' How the hell am I supposed to know? It's sailing – it depends on things I have no control over.

Arriving anywhere is always a miracle, an achievement. But for a skipper, there's no time to relax. The first thing to do is redo all the warps that the crew haven't tied properly before they scamper off to the Deserter's Arms (I couldn't even make out what one of them shouted from the other end of the pontoon). Of course, you mustn't mention it otherwise they'll accuse you of being 'overcritical, 'a control freak' or 'a megalomaniac psychopath'. And all because you had a bit of an issue about wanting your boat still to be there when you get back.

Not that you'll be away for long. While they're on their second pint, I'm still on board trying to figure whether we've got enough water under us so we don't dry out, what tomorrow's tides are doing and when we have to leave so they can all get back home in time, otherwise they'll moan even more. Before joining them in the bar, you still have to go to the harbourmaster's office to pay for your berth and get the weather outlook.

Only then can you relax. You walk into the bar – and if the barman hasn't already called time, the bastards expect you to buy them a drink!

LESSONS NOT LEARNED

Like you, I'm pretty reasonable, so when I tell you everyone I've sailed with has been entirely unreasonable I know I'm not alone. In fact, everyone I know has the same trouble. One solution for skippers is to masquerade as some kind of solo Buddhist vegetarian sea mystic like Bernard Moitessier – but not Bernard Moitessier – and sail alone; then you'd have no one to moan about. Problem is, though, who would you moan to about that? As for crew, what would we have to talk about on runs ashore, and how would we bond and plot mutiny without skippers? Come to think of it, why disturb the status quo? The existing arrangement works just fine. It's the way of the sea.

~~ELVIS~~ IN MY SHROUDS

In a certain light I swear I can see an impression of Elvis's face.

Made it! It's late May and at last *Marlin's* back in the water. It wasn't so much a team effort, more an international relief operation. My 18-foot polyester blob is once more merrily bobbing on her mooring, a hideous visual affront to the aesthetic sensibilities of the old gaffers who ply the Blackwater in smocks, kerchiefs and oatmeal beards garnished with wood chips, tar and dribble. That's pleasure enough in itself, but soon I'll be out there causing all kinds of complications to east-coast navigation. I can't wait.

When I took *Marlin* out of the water last October, she was fine; one trailer tyre had a slow puncture that wasn't fast enough to bother me and everything else seemed pretty much all right. But as the winter months passed, my old mischievous mentors Julian and Ted, who have taken me on as a nautical care-in-the-community project

(I suspect they get an EU grant for it), started planting subversive thoughts in my head. I've come to learn that this is their chief pleasure in life.

Julian resumed his familiar old 'Might one suggest...' routine, a gentle subliminal drip-feed that always develops into irresistible and intolerable water torture. This time the suggestion was that my genoa was 'a little tired', or 'perhaps past its best', or 'might be donated to the National Maritime Museum'. As far as I was concerned it seemed fine. OK, it had stretched to the point where you couldn't see round it or under it, but that's not a problem when you can see through it. What's more, in certain lights I'd swear you can see an impression of Elvis's face in it and sometimes there's even a tear rolling down his cheek. This is one of the things that makes sailing such a humbling spiritual experience for me.

In the end, though, I cracked and ordered a spanking new genoa from Arun, who originally made the Sailfish sails and still have all the patterns. They weren't interested in my old genoa in part exchange, so I'll probably cut it into centimetre squares and sell it on eBay as 'Ye True Shroud of Elvis'.

Meanwhile, the devious duo had been making opaque asides about 'winterising' my mighty Mercury 3.3hp two-stroke to prevent apocalyptic things from happening. Eventually I gave a bloke some money and months later as spring arrived I asked Julian and Ted about 'summerising' my engine. All they did was snigger as they made sly whispered exchanges behind their hands. This kind of help just doesn't help.

Their next trick was a masterstroke. They took one look at *Marlin's* chalky, crumbling rubbing strip and started pulling it off. It took about 30 seconds, but left my poor boat mutilated with hundreds of tiny screw-hole wounds that all needed filling. Who'd have thought that for an 18-foot boat you'd need half a mile of

fendering, thousands of stainless-steel screws and several million fiddly little plugs, all cut by hand and glued individually into holes.

It was early May by the time I got *Marlin* on the foreshore ready to launch at Stone Sailing Club – a miracle in itself, what with all the help and guidance over the previous months. Then there was one more hiccup: I couldn't quite remember where my mooring was. So I inflated my tender and went for a look – but there was no sign of buoy 55.

Over the winter a number of buoys had gone missing; whether the cause was storms, propellers, thieves or the supernatural, no one knows for sure? One of those things.

It was then that the Stone Sailing Club task force came to my aid. And the amazing thing is that, unlike International Rescue, you don't even have to call these supermen in galoshes. Whenever you're in trouble, Roy and Stan just seem to materialise – I suspect they might be using a secret network of wartime underground tunnels with hidden hatches behind sheds and under piles of tyres. And instead of Thunderbirds 1 and 2 they operate a workboat and a tractor.

They kindly dragged the seabed for any remains of my mooring, but came up with nothing. It was then that Rolex Sam, the moorings clerk, came sauntering round a corner in his moleskin-collared overcoat (I don't think he uses tunnels, more likely a Jag) and offered to 'do' me sinkers, risers, shackles, a Rolex, chains, thimbles, multiplait, a Rolex, nylons, conservatory, a Rolex, and tarmac my driveway.

I opted for Sam's nautical stuff and with a rummage in Roy and Stan's garages for second-hand gear I had everything I needed for my mooring. The only thing is I didn't have a clue how to put it together – but over the next week Roy took care of it all, and

when I arrived back at Stone the three-quarter-ton concrete sinker with all the tackle had been lifted by tractor to the low-water line. A couple of hours later on the rising tide, Roy and Stan – and I myself as a pointless impediment – lifted the mooring and towed it into position.

An hour or two later, bang on high water, Roy was behind the wheel of the tractor, pushing me, my boat and my trailer into the water. With a final nudge *Marlin* floated off.

I turned to shout my thanks, but Roy had already gone – who knows where? But somehow you can be sure that whenever there's a need he'll materialise again – from behind a diesel drum or a pile of driftwood … this galoshed crusader!

LESSONS NOT LEARNED

My new Rolex has made my wrist go green. And do you know why Rolex owners are so sociable? They have to keep asking each other the time. Mind you, mine keeps perfect time – must be a fake. And it didn't cost much more than a genuine one, which doesn't cost much more than my new mooring tackle. However, sailing is a lifestyle choice, and has provided Rolex Sam with an enviable one … and a very large boat.

SINGLE-HANDED –
ALONE,
ALL BY MYSELF

The harbourmaster noticed I was single-handed...

At last *Marlin* was launched. But what now? I'd been lying to one of the scrubbing posts off Stone Sailing Club for at least an hour, tidying things up and generally faffing about.

In truth, though, what I was really doing was crapping myself. I had a big decision to make. The sky was ugly, and the wind scudded across the wide expanse of an empty Blackwater, which is usually a cheerful riot of technicolour sails. And all the while, the sucking ebb gathered force and laid man-size buoys over on their side as they gulped for breath. This force seemed more than

nature, as if the Creature from the Black Lagoon was dragging them under to claim as baubles to brighten his slimy grotto.

I had two options: I could motor over to my mooring buoy, tie up, go home and be warm and dry; or I could show a bit of character and go for my first sail of the season. The truth is I was scared. I felt as if I'd never sailed before and my judgement was all haywire. I was so out of touch with my environment, all I could tell was that the wind was somewhere between force 3 and 10 – probably. Yet, inside I felt that if I didn't set sail now I never would again.

But with each minute that passed a third – and very inviting – possibility began to seep into my dazed consciousness. Do nothing! Then in an hour or so *Marlin* would take the ground and I could walk ashore, stroll to the bar and say, 'Aw shucks, what a pity, I really felt like going for a sail.' Although all the honest sailors of Stone Sailing Club would see straight through my phoney bravado, I was beginning to find myself pretty convincing.

I don't know whether I consciously chose any course of action, but in a moment someone's disembodied hands had set *Marlin* free while another pair snatched at the engine starter cord. As the buzz of the mighty Mariner 3.3hp brought me back into the world I saw my mooring ahead. A few moments later and it was receding in our wake. Someone – or something – had made a decision.

The rest is a tangled blur. The mainsail was hoisted, double reefed, but *Marlin* was lying beam on to the wind and the main sheet was trailing free and unraveling into the water at the end of the boom. I'd forgotten to tie a stop knot. Each time I reached for the boom and pulled it in, the boat powered up and pulled the boom out of my grip. One, two, three, four times I tried.

In a rare moment of lucid thought I throttled up the mighty Mariner and just about managed to bring her round into the wind and snatch the end of the main sheet as the boom swung for me. Next, unfurl two tads of genoa, kill the engine and we're off – sailing again.

I'd even had the presence of mind to attach myself to a safety line. Now relax. Get the feel of her again ... but it all feels so strange. Doh, you dummy! No wonder, the topping lift's still on. Got that sorted. Now relax – something's still not right. Doh! I forgot the kicking strap.

At last, now we're sailing – but where to? The wind's in the south, I'm flailing east on the ebb out of Blackwater estuary. Next stop France, Belgium, Holland, Germany, Denmark or Norway – but I haven't got the charts and I'll never make it on two date-expired Cup-a-Soups. Brightlingsea it will have to be, then.

Now it's raining, sheeting down. I'm still in shorts and barefoot from launching and the cockpit's filling up. On the positive side, though, I'm not ruining a good pair of shoes.

At least my charts and VHF are dry; they're triple-wrapped in carrier bags in the bottom-most recesses of my waterproof kit bag which is stuffed in the darkest, tiniest, most inaccessible fissure found on a Sailfish. I remember how to heave-to and go below for a wrestling session.

Next, sails down, fenders out, mooring lines, call Brightlingsea harbourmaster. Then, very, very, very proud moment. As the harbourmaster's launch guides me to a berth and notices I'm single-handed, he says, 'Do you need a hand with the lines?'

I reply, super-casual, 'No, I'll be fine, thanks.' How they must wonder at my seamanship. Once they're out of sight I ram the

pontoon and settle down for a cup of tea feeling quietly proud of myself.

Then 'dry' John, who handles his water-taxi with the pinpoint poise of a ballerina on points, but whose real job is to look faintly amused by the cock-ups of weekend sailors, motors up and says, 'All alone, then?'

Aah, I think, recognition at last from a real, proper working boatman. I nod as I imagine Hemingway might and the caustic cabbie says, 'You're slipping. Last time you had two birds on board!'

If only I'd had more Cup-a-Soups I could have gone to Norway to be insulted.

LESSONS NOT LEARNED

Solo sailing impresses no one, unless you're Ellen MacArthur, Robin Knox-Johnston or Bernard Moitessier. I've modelled myself on the latter, whose particular blend of bare-footed romantic French vegetarian mysticism and chunky knitwear proved irresistible to women. This doesn't work in Brightlingsea ... or on a Sailfish.

AN EXTREME NARROW-WATER CHALLENGE

'Oh yes, Sir... The look is so Fastnet.'

'It was the biggest challenge of my life, we were really pushing the envelope on this one, yes of course there were the highs and lows and the clock never stops ticking, it pushed me further than I thought I could go, but the boat looked after me and I feel we've really raised the bar. At the end of the day it was a team effort, the weather routers, IT guys and comms people all performed at 11/10ths, so all I had to do was sail the boat. But when I had that trouble with the kettle it was the incredible support of the general public that kept me going – that and the cuddly toy my mum stowed away (I later threw it overboard to improve boat speed, but don't tell her). I feel very emotional right now, blub, blub (can you see my lower lip quivering?), but I would just like to thank all the guys at Kleenex who supplied my offshore tissues, Corp. Inc. Ltd

for all the dosh and Acme Fancy Goods (Leyton High Road) for all the bits that broke, giving me an endless supply of sound bites...'

Something's happened to me. I've done a couple of races and I've changed. All of a sudden I've been struck down with that rare offshore affliction known as Ellen-speak. In the near past I would simply have said, 'Fine, thanks,' but now when people ask, 'How are you?' the barrage above is my more usual response.

It gets worse. Racing has also had a catastrophic effect on my physical appearance. I now wear Oakley wraparound reflective sunglasses all the time, even when I'm not in nightclubs; my hair has suddenly gone all spiky with little blond peaks and crests – like a baked Alaska; and I wear thongs – footwear, not underwear – to all formal occasions, even in winter. It's my interpretation of the laid-back don't-give-a-stuff surfer-dood look favoured by intense competitors like rower James Cracknell and powerboater Steve Curtis.

I've adopted this anti-corporate look to offset the alphabetti spaghetti of sponsor logos on my shirt, which is the kind of all-purpose fashion crossover item that could be worn by a Formula One pit crew moonlighting as a bowling-alley attendant in *Happy Days*.

It's not an image I'm altogether happy with, but it helps underpin the delusions of adequacy that have infected me as a result of my racing exploits.

Until June, the only racing I had ever done was as crew in a couple of the chilly Frost Bite races, from Limehouse to Erith and back on the Thames. I hated them. All that happened was that my mild-mannered pal Julian went bazonkers, shouting, 'IN-IIN-IIIN-IIIIN-IIIIIN!' followed instantly by 'OUT-OUUT-OUUUUT-OUUUUT-OUUUUUT!' I was on the genoa sheet, and if only

he'd occasionally said 'Stop' or 'That's enough' he wouldn't have made himself hoarse and I wouldn't have wasted so much effort yo-yoing the genoa in and out all the bleedin' time.

In June I met up with other Sailfish folk at the Cam Sailing Club, a club founded in 1899 and so beautifully preserved in Famous Five aspic it makes you ache for the childhood you never knew. I wondered whether, like *Brigadoon* – the Gene Kelly, Cyd Charisse Hollywood romance – this idyllic club with its picture-perfect period chalets arranged in a crescent round a lush lawn groomed by period-perfect, fluffy, grass-nibbling bunnies was an apparition that arose from the mists just once every hundred years.

I was crewing for sprightly octogenarian Theo Stanley, whose Sailfish bristles with so many modifications I'm surprised it never appeared on *Tomorrow's World*. Curiously, I've got no recollection of Saturday's race result, but I won't forget the idyllic scenes of weeping willows leaning over to tickle their reflection in the river, ducks and drakes fussily herding their fluffy battery-powered chicks, the haughty swans so certain of their own pristine, dazzling white beauty and long-lashed pop-up-book cows lapping at the water's edge.

Obviously I'd lacked focus, but Sunday was a different matter. We really started to gel as a team and decided to 'push the envelope'. Theo had me poling out the genoa with the boathook and shifting my bulk forward and aft, port and starboard, to trim the boat. In idle moments he introduced me to further modifications including the car-window winding motor which lowers the keel, and every now and then he told me that his GPS said we were anywhere between 3903 and 3910 miles from Key Largo in Florida. Useful to know.

Meanwhile, this racing lark was beginning to awaken a dormant competitive streak in me. I'd noticed that we were now a whole

river bend ahead of the nearest boat – in other words, if we started the engine they'd never know. Theo's reaction to my suggestion was rather abrupt so I assured him I was only joking. Pity, really, 'cos we won the race, but with my innovative strategy I feel we could have 'really raised the bar' and perhaps even tempted Dame Ellen to take a crack at the Cam, although her 'tri' would have to be heavily modified into a 'mono' – or perhaps 'minnow' – for this extreme narrow-water challenge.

As for me, I'm off to do the rounds of corporate sponsors – but I must admit the prospects are limited. Owing to my Sailfish's modest proportions I've only got room for B&. The Q will have to go on the other side.

LESSONS NOT LEARNED

walk the walk and talk the talk and no one will ever understand a word you say ever again. This is how you become a motivational speaker. This kind of talk also empties all waterfront pubs in the civilised world. In the Hamble, it fills them. In the Queen's Head in Maldon, Essex, landlady Viv has banned race-speak. It's bad for business. Acceptable subjects are smacks, barges, the latest developments in coracle design, wildfowling, the war (the 1914-18 one), smuggling, the flood of '53, the big freeze of '61 and the war (the 1939-45 one).

THE IMPOSSIBILITY OF RESISTING THE MENTAL DECAY AND DECADENCE OF PONTOON LIFE

'I did say not to overload the trolley, dear – it's low water springs.'

There's one call of nature more ghostly, ghastly and woebegone than a curlew's haunted cry. It came the other day across the water, this eerie, desperate plea. 'What's the c-o-o-o-o-d-e?' was the plaintive, disembodied howl that snatched at the wind and then died, never to be answered. The realisation was chilling. I was in a marina!

With a stiff force 2½ blasting down from the Arctic I felt I could be here for days. Any more than a week and I'd have a big decision to make, for by then the berthing fees would have outstripped the value of my little tub and I'd have to think seriously about doing a runner.

Still, what a marina does give you is access to undreamed-of luxuries and the chance to glimpse another side of sailing life. The trouble is, spend too long in one and your mind starts to go to mush.

The code for the toilet and shower block was easy enough to remember – at first. A big bloke in those faded tan – i.e. pink – canvas trousers that men in Fulham and south-coast yacht clubs think don't look gay told me it was the harbourmaster's wife's chest measurement, followed by his mistress's waist – both figures with which local men seemed to be comfortably familiar – then a Z. I don't know why, but there's always a Z.

Inside, a miraculous scene of steaming Pompeiian decadence unfolded before me, real flushing toilets and water that came from taps; it was even clear, unlike the lumpy green gloop that comes out of a hose. The greatest wonder was the showers; not only were there doors on the cubicles; the water was actually hot, as in not cold. This was livin'.

The only unsavoury aspect was the hideous vision of acres of half-naked men, four ruddy cheeks apiece, towelling themselves down vigorously – and all whistling in an awkward, mock-casual manner, not just any tunes, but manful ones like the theme from *The Bridge on the River Kwai*, *633 Squadron* or *The Dam Busters*. If you wanted the place all to yourself, all you'd have to do is hum a Lloyd-Webber show tune.

I adopted *The Great Escape* as my marina theme, little realising the poignant irony.

But there's more to marina life than shower blocks. Wherever you're moored, between your boat and the showers there's always a chandlery that cunningly lures you in by also selling milk and papers. Pretty soon, the magnetic pull of glittering objects is

too powerful to resist, and in the same hypnotic trance that draws Homer Simpson to Duff Beer there's a constant voice in your head saying, 'Must buy shiny objects, must buy shiny objects.' Pretty soon you've draped the entire interior of your boat with snap-crackle-shackle-buckle thingies that glitter at you.

By now you're losing touch with nature and each time you look up at your limp ensign you judge that it's giving the lie to the hurricane conditions on the other side of the marina wall and that only a fool would go out in such a blow.

It's just as well, really, as there's so much to do. All over the marina, little men with gnarled-oak knees are trudging up and down pontoons, trundling gigantic trolleys full of boaty stuff. Some of them have even got boats; for the others it just gives them a sense of belonging. And all the while, there are 'projects' going on. There's nothing much to see, but you can hear the whirr of drills, the whizzing screech of belt sanders, the buzzing jig-saws and any other power tools that consume huge amounts of marina electricity. Resonating from within the GRP hulls there's a percussive accompaniment of banging, thumping and rasping hand tools, punctuated at regular intervals by agonised torrents of expletives. This is the song of the marina.

I've got my own projects in mind, but the trouble is there's so much to do and for some reason everything's taking longer. When I'm on my boat and unconnected to land there's nothing to forget – either it's all there, or it isn't. Life's simple.

But this pontoon living is a different matter. I'm having trouble getting to the shower block without forgetting my flannel, soap or towel, and then forgetting something else on the way back. Two journeys become four and, of course, on each one I have to stop at the chandlery for 'shiny things'. Forget your credit card and that's more journeys. How do marina sailors ever find time to go sailing?

Then it happens. I'm jabbing at the keypad and the door won't open. All I can remember is the Z, everything else is a blank – my childhood, breakfast, the rest of the code, it's all gone. Why can't all codes just be Z? 'What's the c-o-o-o-o-d-e?' I cry into the night as I slump to the ground.

It's only then that I realise what's happened to me. If I don't get out quick I'll have to sell my house to pay for a full-time care berth in a 'code-locked, sheltered marina environment'.

And, frankly, what's so terrible about that? There's plenty to do, and the moment I get notification of my pontoon's postcode I'll be sending off for seed catalogues and planning my first planting for next spring's Pontoons in Bloom competition.

LESSONS ~~NOT~~ LEARNED

If marina malaise sets in, embrace it and accept the inevitable. Sell your mast, sails, blocks, winches, shackles, anchor, charts, rudder and anything to do with sailing. They're superfluous. Then you'll be able to pay for your berth and if you get a gardening job tending the primroses and leeks in the dinghy planter outside the chandlery, eventually you'll be able to save up for a mast, sails, blocks, winches, shackles, anchor, charts, rudder and other nautical ephemera that make a boat look ever so boaty. By then you'll be too old to sail, so sell it at a huge loss, buy a narrowboat and remove the engine to finance your lifestyle. Tattoo the marina code on to your palm, and repeat the process 'til the end of eternity.

SCALING NEW HEIGHTS AND PLUMBING THE DEPTHS

Apparently, the sculptor was inspired on a walk beside the River Blackwater.

SAILFISH (INTERRUPTED)

In my own quiet, unassuming way I had completed my firs circumnavigation earlier in the season. Without fanfare, flashbulbs o book deals I'd sailed my own solitary course and circumnavigated Ose Island by the Great Circle route (that'll be about four miles). Yet stil felt a groaning emptiness.

The River Blackwater was my oyster, but what more could this Hobb universe made of gloop offer my restless soul?

And as I sailed alone back downriver from Maldon on a Sunday afternoo in early September, a thought gnawed at me. This was the highest tic

for 20 years, and seeing as that happens only about once every 20 years I decided I really ought to mark the occasion with some kind of entirely pointless superhuman epic exploit.

As I chatted away to some folk sailing alongside, the opportunity suddenly presented itself. There was the back way round Northey Island opening up close by. I'd always imagined those poles at either end of the causeway held power cables. But no. The moment I saw there was clear air between the poles I felt another circumnavigation coming on – and I went for it.

I waved my new friends goodbye and chuckled to myself. As I'd be sailing just the short side of a triangle, they'd be gobsmacked when I somehow appeared ahead of them on the downriver side of Northey Island. But I never got to see their looks of awestruck wonder and reverential respect.

Instead, with an ever so gentle bump, my Sailfish came to a stop. No worries. Going aground is something the Sailfish excels at. Wind the keel up and away you go. Over the last couple of years my bump-and-go method of sailing has become so routine I barely give it any thought – except this time I should have.

After a few more bumps and deft winds of the keel, the next stop, about 20 yards on, was different. This time there was no keel left to wind up. I wouldn't say I panicked but to an untrained observer that could be what it looked like. By pushing off with my tender's oars as hard as I could I got afloat again. Now I could see these little tufts of land all around me just below the water's surface. I lurched over a few more hillocks by climbing off the boat and manhandling her. Then there was nothing more I could do, except watch the water go away and slowly reveal the tufts transforming into islets, mounds, hillocks and downright mountains in the labyrinth of the saltings.

When I looked back from where I'd started I was pretty impressed by how far into the maze I'd managed to get. How high, too. In fact there was a bloke with two dogs on the hillock next to mine, asking, 'How did you get up there?' I mumbled something about the 'highest tide, 20 years, all under control', and he said, 'Mmm, I never realised the water got that high,' and walked off. He was the first of a steady stream as the scene became more and more surreal. *Marlin* was so far out of the water, we looked more like an art installation than anything to do with sailing.

Normally I'd try to save face, by perhaps getting the anti-fouling out and nonchalantly whistling as I slapped a coat on, but I was just too sapped.

My own words were also coming back to haunt me: *highest tide for 20 years!* What if I'd gone aground at the highest point of the highest tide for 20 years – I'd be here for another 20 years. If nothing else, the endless questions of dog-walkers would eventually do me in.

I'd earlier laid a kedge out with my tender and then slept fitfully as I waited to find out if the water would ever come back as high. Shortly after 3 in the morning I tugged at the kedge, and *Marlin* floated free. I pulled her into deep water and waited for the ebb to reveal the tops of the tufts and show my route out.

It was just my luck that the darkest night in time was also the foggiest. I floated in a terrifying space, somewhere between imagination and madness, as wispy plumes of fog drew the faces of murdered seamen aboard skeleton ships on the velvet blackboard of fear.

Too scared and disoriented to sail, I allowed the tide to guide me down the river until the pale sun lifted the heavy lid of reluctant

dawn. I knew I'd have to take the ground again and wait out another tide. Finally, at 4 o'clock on Monday afternoon, I made my mooring and rowed ashore to be welcomed by Stone Sailing Club stalwart Tony.

'Long weekend?' he asked.

'Yeah, kind of,' I replied.

'Ah well, it's happened to us all at some time.'

What did he mean? I popped into the toilets to find out if my hair had turned entirely white. I couldn't tell. I was covered from head to foot in mud – and humility.

LESSONS ~~NOT~~ LEARNED

RYA courses tell you about things like charts and tide tables; charts tell you about things like land; tide tables tell you about things like tides. I've done courses; I have charts and tide tables. They work best if you have them on board. RYA courses didn't mention that. It's the RYA's fault.

SHAKEN AND STIRRED
BY A VISIT TO THE SECRET WATERS OF THE EAST COAST

I don't want to appear a snob, but anyone who's anyone knows the Sailfish Annual Rally is the highlight of the social season. If you doubt me, just ask yourself why the Henley Regatta never clashes with it. 'Nuff said.

This year's bash took place in August at Suffolk Yacht Harbour on the Orwell, and Sailfish folk had come from as far away as miles – literally – trailing their GRP blobs to what must surely be one of the east coast's top-50 most glamorous Tupperware conventions. Trouble is I'm terrified of trailing – it's the only thing that scares me more than sailing (and mushrooms and raw tomatoes, come to think of it) – and I decided to do something quite radical: arrive by water, in my boat, solo. I've got to say I'm really touched by how all my kind friends who've sailed with me have warmly encouraged me to sail alone. I never realised, until now, how supportive they are.

But as I sat the weather out, wet, cold and storm-bound in Brightlingsea, I had my doubts and gloomily imagined the heady

social whirl of taffeta and tuxedos that was going on without me. I'd even inked a sail-tie black to wear as a bow tie on the more formal evenings, but all I could do was sit and wait for the weather to break.

Eventually I decided I had to go for it. It was a considered decision; on the hard a bearded bloke in a fishing smock studied the sky and then said sagely, 'Aaargh, when sky is like a speckled hen, 'tis time to get going then, aaargh.' Plus there was a hooligan swan that had been nibbling at my Sailfish for days and was now getting dangerously – and threateningly – addicted to the taste of osmosis.

With a reef in and the wind aft of the beam I bowled up the coast. This was the first time I'd understood what surfing was and I didn't like it, that out-of-control feeling as the rudder goes light and you're lifted by an invisible hand that suddenly chucks you forward and sends you slewing down the face of a wave; it's like riding a wild tea-tray toboggan that's been kicked downhill by a bully's Doc Marten.

Along the east-coast riviera, past the sophisticated delights of Clacton and Walton, I thought I could hear the roulette wheels spin and chatter in the dazzling playgrounds of the incontinent as *Marlin* hurtled onwards. At the very least I was pretty sure I could smell battered sausages. But the wind was rising and coming forward of the beam. Soon it was east of north, bang on the nose, and I was flailing around off Harwich and Felixstowe – which just happens to be the busiest container port in England, with great big bastards coming from all directions. A gust flipped my tender, its transom digging in and stopping me from tacking; I was over-canvassed but the boat was pitching too violently for me to attempt to put a second reef in; plus, it would be dark soon and *Marlin* has no navigation lights. On the plus side I wasn't wearing sunglasses. Other than that, everything was perfectly under control. And all the while the movers and shakers of the Sailfish world were sipping tea from the finest melamine – while *Marlin*

and I were being shaken and stirred, as mountainous, frothing crests the colour of builder's tea threatened to collapse on us.

There was only one thing to do. Trouble was I didn't know what. I was clutching at straws. For some reason, maybe intuition, I furled my genoa and fired up the mighty Mercury 3.3. This turned out to be pure genius. My engine is on the port side of the transom and with the boat heeling over so much I could only keep the prop in the water on starboard tack. The result: a perfect course into the sanctuary of the Walton Backwaters.

Then, as *Marlin* reached the shelter of the channel, the wind dropped, the seas subsided and the setting sun warmed my world and smiled on one of the east coast's most enchanted places.

So what if the powerbrokers of the upper echelons of Sailfish society were quaffing Bollinger, beluga caviar and Bourbon biscuits without me. That could wait. I had this. In a magical endless moment of eternity I watched the shadows stretch as the sun sank low, then laid its head on a marshy pillow in that bewitched and magical labyrinth of dreams, the neverland and neversea of Arthur Ransome's *Secret Water*.

Then I opened *The RYA Book of Knots* to find out how to do a bow tie.

LESSONS NOT LEARNED

There are lots of bearded blokes in fishing smocks in Brightlingsea. Don't listen to them ... especially if they talk in rhymes. They're folk singers and Morris dancers. The RYA does courses that teach you about things like weather forecasts. Weather forecasts can be found on harbour-master's noticeboards and on the VHF and radio. These work best if you look at them or listen to them. The RYA never mentioned that on my course. It's the RYA's fault.

THE SLOW BOAT TO WOODBRIDGE

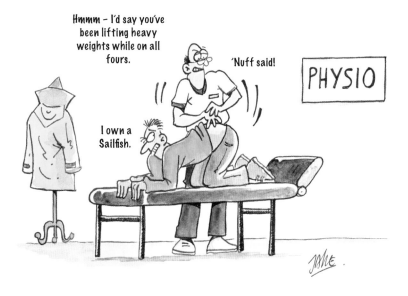

Four days into my annual holiday and I was beginning to feel I could really – I mean really – do with a holiday. In fact, if you'd offered me a fortnight in any of the destinations featured in those 'Holiday Hell' TV programmes I'd have jumped at it.

The plan had been to join the Sailfish Annual Rally for lazy, hazy days of leisure and high livin'. But it hadn't worked out like that. After three days stuck in the departure lounge, waiting out the foul weather, I had taken off on a terrifying solo flight up the east coast in my Sailfish. The trouble was I hadn't exactly touched down in the right resort. I'd bolted into Titchmarsh marina in the Walton Backwaters, while all the serious Sailfish socialising was going on 12 miles away at Suffolk Yacht Harbour on the River Orwell.

I put in a call to Peter Stratford, Sailfish Tours' local rep, and he said, 'We were getting a bit worried about you – it was five, six gusting seven off Felixstowe.'

I was concerned. For a start, I swear I could hear a bouzouki playing and plates smashing in the background on his end of the line. Second, I knew it had been rough out there – I gathered that much when my tender flipped – but I was shocked to learn how bad. All at once I felt stupid, proud and brave.

Stupid, because I really shouldn't have been out there (I really need to try and get some understanding of the weather over the winter); proud, because my brilliant little Sailfish had performed amazingly and really looked after me; and brave – 'cos I'm stupid.

Peter suggested we rendezvous off Felixstowe Pier and head up the Suffolk coast to the River Deben. Four hours later I was hove-to off the pier, alone with my thoughts, pondering yesterday's dumb exploits and musing as to which sounded better – 'Offshore' Dave or Dave Knox-Selby? There was also another thought as I watched *Marlin* close the coast, and that was that heaving-to seems to be faster than sailing – at least the way I do it. Curious!

In the distance I could see my Sailfish buddies approaching and, all puffed up with solo-sailor conceit, I reckoned I'd converge with them somewhere in the middle order and then majestically surge to the front of the pack. We soon got into a routine whereby they all hove-to, waited for me to catch up and overtake, put their kettles on for a cuppa, quickly overhauled me again and then hove-to again to wait patiently for me catch up once more. Sometimes to vary it they just sailed in circles for a bit.

The entrance to the River Deben is notorious for its shifting bar, so much so that there are several websites to inform mariners of the latest whereabouts of the channel. Another way to approach it is to make sure that you're at the back of a convoy and follow the others in. And when I saw the crews of the boats ahead 'assume the Sailfish position' in the companionway I knew from their body language that there wasn't an awful lot of water under the lifting keel. The Sailfish position, by the way, is the stance required for just about any activity aboard a Sailfish, from boiling a kettle to dropping anchor, and involves kneeling on all fours with your bum sticking up in the air. On this occasion the Sailfish crew had assumed the position to wind their keels up rather smartly.

The winding Deben is certainly the most beautiful river I've ever seen, and as we wafted upriver there was a quiet pleasure in the knowledge that our Sailfish flotilla was causing a momentary stall in property values as we blighted the prospects of the million-pound riverside dwellings.

By the time we got to the Tide Mill at Woodbridge it had been a long day on the water for me – 12 hours and about 25 miles, in fact – but I'd finally made it. I was on holiday. I lit my barbecue, prised open a beer, kicked back and spent the evening chatting away and listening to kindly explanations as to why my boat is slower than the rest. All the well-meant suggestions were perfectly plausible – rig tension, weed growth etc. – but I knew the real truth.

Stuff those grandiose Dave Knox-Selby notions. The explanation was simple. These Sailfish folk really know how to sail their boats. That's all. And I was beginning to learn how little I know. This holiday was going to be an education.

LESSONS NOT LEARNED

RYA courses teach you about things like sailing. Sailing involves pulling ropes and stuff. To preserve delusions of adequacy it's best never to sail with other boats exactly the same as yours. The RYA doesn't teach you that. It's the RYA's fault.

HEADING OFF INTO THE WIND AND RAIN
SEEMED LIKE A GOOD IDEA AT THE TIME...

I felt completely depleted and slumped at the tiller.

JAKE.

Normally, when I enter a marina, the first thing I do is check the damage to the pontoon, then go and apologise to the boats I've hit on the way in. But for once that could wait, for there before me, as I drew alongside, was a hand proffering a gorgeous, steaming, beautiful mug of tea. In fact, it was more than tea.

It was a symbol, the Holy Grail at the end of my quest, my Golden Fleece, everything I'd hoped for, and more, as I'd pursued my Homeric odyssey to join the Sailfish Annual Rally. At times, its elusive steaming promise was all that had kept me going as I battled up the coast, dived for cover into the Walton Backwaters, made a detour to Woodbridge on the Deben and, finally, reached my goal, arriving at Suffolk Yacht Harbour on the River Orwell five days after the rally started. We are talking serious passagemaking here, about 80 miles or so (that's an average of 16 miles a day), sometimes as far as a whole mile offshore. Epic.

In the end I'd finally made it. And I don't mind telling you, the tea flowed endlessly. For days to come, whenever any of the other Sailfish folk ventured 'Tea at my place,' I shot off down the pontoons like a tannin-crazed terrier, to gorge on an endless orgy of tea, accompanied by Custard Creams, Bourbons, Garibaldis and other 1970s-style fancies, fittingly chosen as homage to the glory years of the Sailfish.

But it couldn't last. With a miserable weather outlook – at least, that was their excuse – the other Sailfish owners decided to end the rally early, load their boats on their trailers and head home for tea.

That left me alone again, waiting out the weather. Each day I listened to the VHF pronounce, 'Grim-to-horrible, becoming worse later, outlook bleak.' On the third day I decided to go for it. The forecast wasn't that much better; I just feared that if I spent another night in my Sailfish I'd never actually stand upright again.

I left just before the dawn and for a brief while felt the great wonder of having the world to myself. Then it went downhill. As I plugged down the coast past Walton and Clacton, the wind headed me, then began to rise. Then came the rain, a machine-gun rat-a-tat-tat of vicious, nasty, hard stinging bullets firing into my face. Next thing, the wind subsides, the sun comes out, I start to poach in my oilskins and peel off my outer layers before I just become mush, like a boil-in-the-bag meal.

It doesn't happen just once, but again and again, and I settle into a grimly repetitive routine: one reef, two, rain, poach, boil-in-the-bag, shake reefs out, strip off, then repeat, and repeat again, and again. Even in the lulls there's no peace – or chance of a cuppa – as *Marlin* is luridly lurching around on the leftovers.

Worse yet, I'm not even getting anywhere. Normally you'd hope to have one making tack, but both of mine are losers. After a while

I'm as bored of seeing Clacton Pier as the fishermen are of seeing an endless procession of faded pale blue Sailfishes, all called *Marlin*!

Inch by inch, I clawed homewards. Then the gods decided to really have fun. As, at last, the faint outline of Bradwell power station came into view at the entrance of the River Blackwater, the wind went ballistic and just for extra fun they threw in bolts of lightning.

I got all the sails down and learned, the hard way, that my mighty Mercury 3.3hp, even at full throttle, couldn't plug through these vicious, short, sharp seas, and for the very first time I felt the thumps and crashes were hurting *Marlin*. Once back under sail, double reefed and close-hauled, the motion was less chaotic as we met the waves at a kinder angle.

Perhaps because I was now back in my familiar home waters, I suddenly felt completely depleted and as the wind began to subside once more I slumped at the tiller. It was the warming rays of the sun that brought me round and, as I looked about me, a rainbow arched over the Blackwater to welcome me home. And for the first time all day the wind, now just a breeze, came round on the beam and caressed *Marlin* on her way. As the rippling wake tickled the tiller in a chuckling song of eternity I wanted this moment to last for ever. Mind you, I could murder a cup of tea.

LESSONS ~~NOT~~ LEARNED

The RYA does courses. These work best if you attend, pay attention, or sit next to the bright bloke. The RYA never explained any of that, so I used my own initiative and asked the bright bloke to sail with me. 'Cos he was bright and had learned lots on the RYA course, he wouldn't. It's the RYA's fault.

DERELICTION OF BEAUTY

I hate the classic boat poseur types

I don't think the government – or the RYA for that matter – are being entirely open when it comes to warning us of the true perils of sailing. If the authorities took their responsibilities a little more seriously, there would be a great big government health warning wrapped round the bottom third of all boat hulls. In unmissable double-extra-bold script it would read 'WARNING: sailing will seriously damage your dress sense.'

Of course, this doesn't apply to Sunseeker owners who, in this respect at least, have a head start, as they spend their entire adult lives in golf wear – even, I'm told, on the golf course. For them, 'slack water' is not a state of tide, but a state of mind dictating that, when you're at sea, slacks must be worn at all times. You may think I'm being unkind, but if you've ever wondered why you never see Sunseeker owners wearing lifejackets it's because Crewsaver don't do them in Burberry check.

It was an out-of-body moment on the Essex foreshore at Stone Sailing Club that brought home to me how, in a just a few short

years, sailing had completely wiped out my dress sense, which was never that highly developed in the first place (I started out a rockabilly and slowly evolved into a sad old Ted). Anyway, it was when I caught myself uttering the words 'What size drain holes do you drill in your galoshes?' that the full realisation of my sartorial dereliction really hit home.

It all started off just three years ago with posh, blue nautical wellies, which I'm told grip really well on teak and GRP – but I never got to find out. However, wearing them to traverse the muddy nursery slopes of the River Blackwater amounted to a full-on death wish as I slithered seaward faster than a kamikaze downhill ski racer with a rocket pack – it's not as easy as it sounds trying to maintain a streamlined tuck position carrying a pair of oars and an outboard.

Those costly blue yotty wellies were an expensive mistake, but they taught me an important lesson. All my subsequent mistakes have been cheaper. Next, either on some course, or perhaps in a bar, someone told me that the only 'sailorly' footwear was wellies two sizes too big; that's so you can kick them off if you fall off your boat. Again, I never found out, but the Mk2 wellies – this time green – did make it as far as the water, just. Three steps in, I stepped out of them as the suction of the mud bottom took hold.

Like the blue Mk1 wellies they were last seen floating downriver towards the cooling-water intake of Bradwell nuclear power station. Briefly I toyed with the idea of using the beneficial effects of mud suction to my advantage by permanently positioning several dozen pairs of green wellies in the shallows to use as sort of stepping – or step-in – stones. As far as I could see, there were only two possible drawbacks: if the wash from passing Sunseekers didn't swamp them, the equinoctial spring tides would.

My next foreshore fashion foray was, I thought, rather bold and quite daring, but ultimately doomed. For one brief tantalising

moment jelly-bean shoes seemed to hold the solution, but my left one came adrift and was last heard of down Bradwell way. The right, along with several dozen other footwear oddments, is in the rear footwell of my car. I hold on to them just in case any of their matching partners floats by someday.

The galoshes, although they gave me self-knowledge, were never really a goer, but at last I seem to have found my fashion feet with super-cheapo Chinese sandals with Velcro fasteners. They look crap, squelch quite a lot and suffer badly from water retention – until you're in a posh carpeted yacht club; then they start to gush, and unless you keep on the move people'll think you're incontinent. But they do one thing no other item of nautical footwear does. They actually stay on. Of course, in fashion terms they are something of a compromise, but so is the rest of me. Coco Chanel once said. 'Fashion fades, only style remains the same.' Well, I like my clothes to fade a lot before I'll wear them sailing. My basic fashion acid test for nautical wear is to ask (a) whether it's too far gone for gardening and (b) whether you'd be too embarrassed to donate it to a charity shop. If the answer to both is yes, then you're well on the way to perfecting your own personal interpretation of nautical grunge chic.

So much more individual, don't you think, than that co-ordinated his-and-hers gear worn by those boutique sailors of the south coast!

LESSONS NOT LEARNED

I've finally twigged - the answer was there all along. You really can combine style with nautical functionality. My old rockabilly brothel-creepers have got to be the ultimate wading footwear. They're stylish, have soles inches thick and are the size of catamaran floats. In fact, it's like having your own personal marina pontoon under each foot. Mine are suede, of course, and blue, naturally, so ever so nautical. At last, I can go sailing without compromising my style.

VIRTUALLY AN ADMIRAL

'You may be a Yachtmaster Examiner, dear, but without glasses you're a menace.'

Some recreational sailors have got so many qualifications I imagine they sleep in gold-braided, breathable offshore pyjamas, clip themselves on to the banisters when they descend to breakfast, and munch their cereal from a nautical non-slip bowl that's been proven in the Southern Ocean and is available mail order with your boat name (nine letters maximum) stencilled on to it. They are steeped in it.

And that's one of the great things about sailing; it offers course junkies endless opportunities for self-improvement – and certificates.

I remember a few years back, when I did my RYA Competent Crew course, there were a couple of blokes on board who were

taking their Day Skipper practical exam. I couldn't believe mere humans could know so much; name any object that you find on a boat, a spoon or a toilet roll for example, and they could call it something else you'd never heard of. These near super-beings didn't do things as mundane as shopping; to endow it with rufty-tufty sailorly gravitas they went 'victualling' – and just in case you actually knew what victualling was they contorted the pronunciation to 'vittlin' ' to be certain you wouldn't have a clue (and I don't mean clew!).

Of course, I was a mere novice then, and had no notion of how important it is to the smooth running of a boat to keep crew in the dark, generally dazed and confused and utterly disoriented. That way there's far less danger of their ever actually doing anything.

However, even more impressive than these bods was the instructor, who combined in one omnipotent being all the best qualities of Hannibal Lecter, Vlad the Impaler and God.

Little did I realise that these boatmates were only two dimensions of the endless diversity of nautical life. Visit any yacht-club bar and you'll soon get an inkling of the infinite layers of social stratification provided by the nautical class system. Indeed there are certain kinds of sailor who aren't happy unless they've discovered your rating on the RYA evolutionary scale. It's like a maritime version of the Top Trumps card game. A Day Skipper's not bad, but it's trumped by a Coastal Skipper; then you get Yachtmaster in varying gradations from shallow end to deep end, inshore, offshore, ocean and rising all the way to Yachtmaster intergalactic fifth-dan black belt.

And once you've got that, Sunsail will let you charter the USS Starship Enterprise – unskippered – although you may want Spock along for the tricky tidal-height calculations.

But that's not the end of the odyssey.

After that you can continue the ascent to immortality through the ranks of instructor, instructor-examiner, examiner-examiner, examiner-instructor – until eventually you become Tom Cunliffe, whose towering stature, leadership and sheer humanity many rate on a par with Captain Kirk. Personally I think Kirk's got a better haircut.

I've done the RYA Day Skipper theory class at night school, and it's brilliant. In fact I reckon there's enough real learning there to last you a lifetime on the water. But there's a certain strain of sailor who feels they have to get every qualification going, fast-tracked in as little time as possible.

The trouble with some of these desperate overachievers is that they're not always that relaxing to sail with, because they usually decide you're going to be instructed whether you like it or not.

I remember one – a particularly overqualified Vulcan shape-changer who'd taken the form of a woman. On the pontoon she surreptitiously loosened my bowline, then shook it vigorously until it came undone. This was to warn me of the follies and dangers of bowlines. From then on, the weekend, supposedly recreational, became an endless round of correction and improvement. Every other second she flashed one of those irritating flash cards at me (she even took them to the pub); she fired endless questions at me and barked. 'WRONG!' even when I was actually right. I hung my tiny torch above my bunk, until she demonstrated in mime how it would swing, hit everybody on the head and kill all of us – dead. In fact everything I did would kill everybody – unless corrected. It was health-and-safety fetishism gone bonkers.

The boat was plastered in Dymo tape messages and in my disturbed dreams I imagined every one of them said 'WRONG'.

It came to a head at the Butt and Oyster pub at Pinmill on the Orwell. When she asked me what I wanted to eat, the words on the blackboard went all blurry and started dancing before my eyes as I groped for an answer. I couldn't speak, I didn't know, but I did know the answer would be wrong, whatever I said.

It was the most wretched weekend I ever spent on a boat.

And so now if anyone tries to play Top Trump qualifications with me I just say, 'I'm virtually an admiral,' and leave it at that. They look at you a bit weirdly, but at least they don't invite you sailing.

LESSONS NOT LEARNED

I'm glad to report that the RYA has been particularly proactive in addressing the concerns raised by this traumatic experience. They're introducing a course for people who've done too many courses. Additionally, in case I ever get trapped in this situation again I've produced my own set of flash cards which provide all the responses you need. These include: STOP!; ENOUGH!; CEASE!; NOT NOW, I'M ON THE TOILET - SORRY, I MEAN HEADS!; I'VE GOT EAR PLUGS IN AND I CAN'T HEAR A WORD!; I'VE LOST THE WILL TO LIVE!; I'VE LOST THE WILL TO DIE!; GET A LIFE!; TAXI!

AN ALL-CONSUMING PASSION

'My cruising range is a bit limited but I can run a dishwasher…'

Ocean crossings can change the very essence of the human soul. I've seen it happen.

If you have a chat with any of these adventurers before they set off on their first big blue-water idyll – all alone with 30 other boats – you'll probably find someone who's no odder than any other average obsessive, monomaniac sailor.

But when they get back, it's not just their horizons that have shifted; their whole mind-set's been whacked out of kilter. Of course, they'll show you the obligatory Ernest Hemingway he- or she-man picture posing with a dorado (the fish, not the air-vent) they caught and pretended they were going to eat. (Incidentally, have you noticed how pissed off the fish looks? That's because the dorado works on a retainer with blue-water rally organisers and gets paid, but not very much, for allowing itself to be caught by every passing Hallberg-Rassy.)

But it's the next pic that really reveals how deeply changed they are. It's the same proud pose, but they're even prouder of this one. As they excitedly jab the photo in your face, they explain in a voice that's bordering on unhinged, 'AND THAT'S ME WITH OUR BATTERY!'

What's happened to them? To use the language of the clinical psychologist, basically they've blown a fuse. When they set out they were interested in things like boats, the sea, new experiences, new cultures and a spot of mild self-discovery. Now, all of that's been replaced by one consuming passion: ELECTRICITY!

Their boats are festooned with wind generators, towing generators, solar panels and – for all I know – treadmills. But it's not enough, so every day they have to run their engines for hours, which means they have to carry loads more diesel. And what with the weight of the extra diesel and all the other equipment that makes or consumes electricity, the boat sits lower in the water, doesn't sail as well, so needs to motor more, which needs more diesel. If it gets critical they can always throw their sails overboard to save weight.

Then there's the rampant electricity consumption of the radar, laptop, curling tongs, satellite phone and VHF – which is used mainly to discuss electricity consumption. Some boats have battery-monitors, but you really need to know how many amps that's discharging, so what you really want is a battery-monitor-monitor. I've even heard of amp diaries – fairly dry reading unless you're really into current affairs.

No wonder they come back changed people, deafened by their engines and traumatised by prolonged electric shock treatment.

Believe me, I do understand. You might think my Sailfish 18 is poles apart, and certainly it hasn't got any electricity as such,

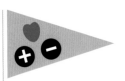

but you wouldn't believe the way it gorges on AA batteries, C cells and PP9s. It really is quite alarming. My last PP9 battery, which powers my Seafarer echo sounder, lasted only three years; at £2.99 that's nearly a pound a year, a considerable outlay in relation to the overall value of a Sailfish.

As for my VHF, I charge that at home; my on-board entertainments system (that's a radio) uses two AAAs; and neither do I have any navigation or anchor lights, although I'm considering some solar-powered wrought-iron-effect pathway/lawn lamps (£6.99 + p&p). At that kind of money I'll probably wait until *PBO* does the definitive 10-product test.

The one area, though, that I just can't get properly sorted is my interior lighting. I've bought a load of those saucer-shaped lights which you press on the front to turn on. The trouble is you need about four to get any decent light – and another four as instant back-up. That's because every 30 seconds or so, either the batteries fail in one or the bulb packs up in another; that leaves you playing quick-action pat-a-cake, a bit like one of those reflex tests, to avoid being plunged into darkness. At the same time I'm holding a torch in my teeth as I race to replace batteries and bulbs in the duff ones. Believe me, I know what stress is.

LESSONS NOT LEARNED

For most of my nautical life I've been 'ohmless', but happy. In fact, I have an inbuilt resistance to change, but technology is moving on apace what with LEDs and wind-up torches and now I think I've finally cracked the problem thanks to the very latest nautical gadget. I've just bought an oil lamp.

A HANDY GUIDE TO GETTING THE MOST OUT OF RACING: AVOID THE RUSH

Disqualified? But I didn't hit a single mark – in fact, I didn't even go round half of them.

Our point exactly.

OYC

If racing is in the blood I must have Horlicks in mine.

When I first started my nautical fumblings on the Blackwater it used to take me a comfortable four and a half hours to ply the 13 miles from Stone to Brightlingsea. More recently I covered the journey in not much over three hours. This worries me. For not only have I conscientiously avoided buying or fitting anything at all that might improve my boat's performance; I've also studiously ignored every article on 'sail-trimming for success' or 'tuning for speed'. Yet somehow I seem to be going faster.

This is no good at all, because as far as I'm concerned the whole reason I go sailing is to slow down, relax and cast off the pressures of everyday life. Getting anywhere quickly simply defeats the whole object. Goddammit, if I was in a hurry I'd walk.

That's why I'd always avoided the cruiser races at Stone Sailing Club – and that was my firm conviction as we sat in the bar one

Saturday evening, watching the sun sink low and the shadows lengthen, while the stories grew taller into the night.

By around 9pm my resolve was just as strong, in the face of a barrage of light-hearted banter and goading. Yet by 9.30 all the bonhomie had evaporated. It seemed only a second later, but it was morning and I was among an audience of grimly intense gimlet-eyed vampires in Musto who, just a few hours before, had pretended to be my friends. This was the race briefing and its purpose, as far as I could see, was to emphasise that racing was not actually a matter of life and death, but more serious than that. The questions and answers merely compounded my terror. For example: 'If he's the stand-on vessel and I'm bigger than him, is it OK if I run him down?' Answer: 'That's a judgement call – depends if anyone's looking.'

The race officer brought the briefing to a close saying, 'Don't forget, it's supposed to be fun.' At that, the throbbing mass of Musto'd malevolence rose up, moved outside and reformed in front of some kind of a drawing or something on the wall. I couldn't tell you what it was because the taller crew had been briefed to stand at the front, to block everyone else's view, while their navigators made notes. Any spare crew were deployed to 'accidentally' stab each other with pencils or rip up each other's notebooks. As proper race etiquette demands, they then said, 'Ooooh, I'm sooo sorry, doncha know!' and stuck their tongues out.

Then, just as suddenly, the living organism dematerialised, reappeared on their boats and started playing nautical chicken in front of the start line.

One thing I've heard said by those racy types who put white lipstick on their lower lip, wear reflective shades and thrash about in the Solent on the corporate hostility race circuit is: 'Yah, to finish first, yah, first you have to finish, yah, ha, ha.'

But that was way too advanced for me. First, I had to start, and as I was solo that involved inflating my tender, rowing out to *Marlin* and then having a major kerfuffle. While I was faffing about I heard the odd gunshot every five minutes or so as the others tried to sink each other. Then I saw Starboard Sam on *Malice Aforethought II* (his brand-new Hades 666) scything through the fleet. Shortly after he'd crossed the start line I heard the blast of someone taking a pop at him, as his constant shrieks of 'Starboard!' (some say it's a tape loop) receded, along with – I'm convinced – the faint strains of Wagner's *Ride of the Valkyries*.

I avoided the rush and got under way about 20 minutes after the start. A few minutes later I saw a numbered yellow buoy and finally figured out that these were the racing marks they'd been going on about; earlier, as part of my kerfuffle, I'd been poring over the chart, trying to figure out why mine showed only green and red ones. Now I understood.

I went round one of the yellow buoys and then another, and it seemed moderately agreeable. Then, further upriver, I heard Starboard Sam on the VHF, advising race control that he was taking a 360-degree penalty turn as he'd passed one mark on the wrong side. Race control replied, 'There's no need, Sam – you're already disqualified for crossing the line before the start.'

It was only then that I understood the unique and extraordinary bond created between sailors by a spot of friendly, competitive yacht racing. For a whole minute, every sailor on the Blackwater with their VHF on channel 37 was lying helpless with laughter in the bottom of their cockpit.

I never realised racing could be so much fun – as long as you're nowhere near the action.

LESSONS NOT LEARNED

For racers who want to get the most of themselves, their boats and their crew the RYA runs special courses in race-craft. I've never been on one 'cos they cost money, but you can acquire all the inside knowledge you need in any sailing club bar. This is what I've learned:

1) Ten minutes before the start, make a VFH announcement on the race channel saying the start has been moved back 20 minutes;
2) Whatever tack you're on, shout, 'Starboard!';
3) If that fails, shout, 'water!';
4) Get the amiable but useless and charming fat bloke on your boat to engage the helm on any nearby boat in meaningless conversation about their mother-in-law's health, pension arrangements or son's progress at uni – their concentration will fall apart and their course will start meandering;
5) Wear reflective sunglasses with the reflective material on the inside; then you'll be able to justifiably claim you're abiding by the Rules of the Road by keeping a lookout at all times without being able to see a thing;
6) Moan about your boat's unfair handicap;
7) Imply that everyone else is cheating;
8) Accuse the race officer of bias and incompetence;
9) Have a brawl in the sailing club bar – this will help you bond and you'll all end up buying each other drinks;
10) Hug all your lifelong mates and tell them, 'You are, hic, me very besht friend, hic, in all the world, hic';
11) Repeat the following week.
There's really not a lot to it. Just to think people go on courses to learn that.

THE MYSTERIES OF MOORINGS

Don't worry – they've only come to 'ley' my mooring.

MOORINGS BY 'DRUID DYNAMICS'

There's more to moorings than you think. **Mine has a life of its own.**

As I walk up the slope behind the sea wall at Stone Sailing Club my pulse always quickens just a bit, in anticipation, hope and a little fear. At the brow, as the vista of the Blackwater estuary spreads out before me, my heart skips – until my eyes have fixed on the faded blue topsides of my beloved *Marlin*, bobbing at her mooring. Relief, she's safe.

A mooring is not just a matter of chain and rope and hope; it's a mystical umbilical cord to mother earth, and the moon that commands the tides. At least mine is – and to make matters worse I think my mooring's been sunk right on a ley line.

From the day I first tied *Marlin* to her buoy, she's been unruly, like a crazed Jack Russell mad angry at being tied up. It seems *Marlin's* possessed of the spirit of my dog Bart. Frankly, the other boats are scared – and they're right to be, for as they bob gently at their moorings, *Marlin* careers wildly about, surging this way and that, yanking at her chain. In her first year she had a nibble at one or two of her mooring mates, and since then *Marlin's* been quarantined,

a leper at the centre of her very own personal exclusion zone that has put all her boat pals out of bounds. *Marlin* only wanted to play.

The waterfront worthies reckon *Marlin's* antics are partly to do with her having the windage of a Portaloo, but I really don't think it's necessary to insult Portaloos just because of their fear of the unknown. One hesitates to use the word 'supernatural', but all the evidence points that way.

Twice in early spring on my first visit of the year I've rowed out to inspect my mooring only to find it gone. The first year I knew I was looking in the right place because I'd done a sailing course and learned how to use transits. The second year I'm not so sure as someone had moved the Transit; it had probably been scrapped.

Again, the naysayers had their theories, suggesting anything from Essex pixies to nuclear subs; some even suggested that the 27 five-gallon plastic cans I'd attached to keep my mooring afloat might have filled with water and actually sunk it. Preposterous!

If you doubt the existence of the supernatural, answer me this. How come, every year without fail, the moment I've realised my mooring's gone, Rolex Sam saunters round the corner with a once-in-a-lifetime offer on all the brand-new kit I'll need to replace my mooring – plus a deal on a Rolex that's guaranteed not to turn your wrist green for three months? That's got to be more than coincidence!

A mooring is an immensely complex thing, part science, part art, part witchcraft. In fact, if you ever wondered why the Egyptians only made pyramids it's because moorings were too difficult. Apart from a three-quarter-ton concrete sinker weight, there's ground chain, risers, multiplait, swivels, rosary beads, shackles, chain pennant, lazy pennant, pickup buoy, mooring buoy and lots of other stuff far too technical for the likes of you to understand.

Fortunately, at our club we've got Roy and Stan, the galoshed gurus of ground tackle. They've made the science of it an art; even so, they're not above invoking a little extra help. More than once I've seen Roy ceremonially anoint the thread of a shackle in goo called Stockholm Tar. At the same time he emits a faint and mysterious muttered incantation, which sounds something like 'bloody expensive'.

Now, I don't think anybody on earth actually knows what Stockholm Tar is, or what it does. As far as I can gather it's some kind of pagan or Druid boat woad that is so powerful the EC tried to ban it. And I reckon if the EC takes it that seriously it's best to have its magic powers on your side.

But there is one mystery even greater than this. This year I bought a new inflatable mooring buoy. What I want to know is this: how come you can buy an inflatable mooring buoy anywhere on this planet, but no one on earth has the valves you need to blow one up – except for Roy? I wonder, is he really one of us or did he bring them from the stars?

LESSONS NOT LEARNED

Transits were touched on briefly in the chapter above, but you ought also to consider marinas. These were invented in the 1970s and while the British Leyland ones disappointed millions of motorists, their essentially static nature led to the name's later adoption as the ideal term to describe boat parking lots. Of course marina berths are expensive, with typical costs per annum amounting to roughly 50 marinas. Mind you, concrete and chain are also pricey. The only cost-effective solution to a permanent mooring buoy is to sink a marina. No one will ever nick it and you'll have the added satisfaction of knowing you've done your bit to save the planet. Austin Allegros also work.

HOW TO PERFECT THE NAUTICAL LOOK AND GET LOTTERY FUNDING FOR IT

'Just a touch more antifoul, a little essence of diesel, and your "I own a Thames barge" ensemble is complete!'

I've moved to Maldon – it's the place where the famous sea salt comes from and, believe me, it is SALTY.

This old town, on the Essex coast at the head of the River Blackwater, is saltier than a barrel full of anchovies marinated in the armpit of a boilerman stoking the fires of hell – in a polyester jumpsuit.

This place is saturated in old salts. In fact it's not just old salts, it takes all salts and that's why I'm hoping I might fit in. It's 38 miles and a world away from my native Stratford, East London, host to the 2012 Olympics, where I reckoned we were bound to win Gold as long as there was a 4x400 mobile-phone snatch. In Stratford you can walk on water; to ford the River Lea, as the Romans did before, just use shopping trolleys and stolen motorbikes as stepping stones.

It's even further too from the world of the south-coast boutique sailor, where marinas are never more than a gin and tonic apart. No, Maldon is authentic, oak-smoked, stove-enamelled, wood-burning and whittled. There's a pecking order here and if I play my cards right, and keep my head down, there's a chance that in time I might aspire to the lowest rung.

This is how it goes. At the top of the pile are the sailing barges, their mighty tan sails dyed with a diluted distillate of the stuff Essex girls use to make themselves orange; next there are the glorious bowspritted smacks, the Ford XR3is of carvel haute couture; then there's anything that's wood; sea-ment comes next, 'cos legendary cartoonist Mike Peyton plies these waters and even land has to give way to his concrete boat – it's the law. Then way down in the bilges of social hierarchy are GRP boats. We are scum.

That's the way it goes. I accept it, but Bart isn't happy, and to tell you the truth I think the little bastard's hampered my chances of social advancement in Maldon. Bart, by the way, is my Jack Russell terrier, a randy criminal mastermind with attention deficit hyperactivity disorder and a talent for credit-card fraud. He hates boats – and everything else.

Unfortunately his arrival in Maldon coincided with the disappearance of a cat from one of the smart barges. Coincidence.

I knew it couldn't be Bart 'cos he's never deigned to take on anything smaller than an artic.

Mind you, Bart's not perfect. For the first three months as we walked along the Hythe each day, Bart religiously lifted a leg and moistened the barge warps on every single bollard on the quay. It was a duty. Far from seeming grateful, men in smocks, kerchiefs and rubber gloves glowered out of hatches at my hound – well, at me, actually, until I finally twigged dogs peeing on ropes is a bit of a no-no in these parts. That's because tradition counts around here, and there are just six local men who have licences to pee on barge warps, on account of an ancient birthright and centuries of genetic evolution which have endowed the pee of these proud marsh men with exceptional preservative qualities.

In any case, they ought to count themselves lucky, 'cos some highly co-ordinated longer-legged mutt had left a steaming 99 plumb-centre on top of a mooring bollard. Now, that's precision. Respect!

Frankly, Bart's an embarrassment, but I'm doing my best to fit in. Maldon has the highest concentration of men with grey beards anywhere on earth; it's the look. This is generally complemented with a pair of 'Empire-made' blue engineering overalls – singed long ago in a boiler-room fire, holed by battery acid and spattered with anti-fouling, which in Maldon is used in place of starch and also provides the overalls with their structural integrity. Next you need a kerchief and a three-legged one-eyed dog the same salt-and-pepper hues as your beard. Finally, to appear really inconspicuous and give the whole ensemble a sense of purpose, you should always be seen whenever out and about carrying a gobbet of wood or some unidentifiable rusty object. Alternatively, if you really want to go the whole way, accessorise with a Seagull outboard. Of course, it weighs several hundredweight but it will help propel you through

Maldon high society – and let's face it, that's more than a Seagull does in water.

I draw the line at the beard and I'll have a think about the modifications to the dog, but I'm going to give it a go, 'cos apparently, if you get the Maldon look just right, you can get a wodge of Heritage Lottery funding just for hanging around the waterfront and looking a bit ambient – or maybe that should be transient.

Anyway, I think we're beginning to make progress. Bart's stopped peeing on barge warps and for the last six months I've been going about my daily business – you know, to the bank, the post office and Tesco – wearing old engineering overalls, with a Seagull tucked under one arm and Bart at my other side, sporting an old kerchief and pretending to limp.

We haven't go lottery funding yet, but visiting south-coast yachtsmen quite often press coins into my palm and say, 'Don't spend it on drink – that's for the dog.'

LESSONS NOT LEARNED

I've tried my best to fit in, but Bart's holding me back. He's got to go...